T0195794

ARMS
AROUND GOD

LINDA LITCHFIELD STRAUSHEIM

WESTBOW
P R E S S®
A DIVISION OF THOMAS NELSON
& ZONDERVAN

WestBow Press books may be ordered through booksellers or by contacting:

WestBow Press
A Division of Thomas Nelson & Zondervan
1663 Liberty Drive
Bloomington, IN 47403
www.westbowpress.com
844-714-3454

ISBN: 978-1-6642-9908-5 (sc)
ISBN: 978-1-6642-9910-8 (hc)
ISBN: 978-1-6642-9909-2 (e)

Library of Congress Control Number: 2023908138

Print information available on the last page.

WestBow Press rev. date: 6/2/2023

I dedicate this book to my family, friends, and pastors, who have been overwhelmingly encouraging; to my mother and father for bringing me into this world; to all the great men and women whose lives have been changed through the amazing blessing of God's transformation.

Introduction — As an elementary child, I always believed in God and trusted His faithfulness, but it was not until I reached adulthood and experienced addiction that I became closer to Him. Out of desperation and through prayer, God answered my prayers in his timing, and I received the most precious blessing of all — transformation. On a cold, snowy, winter night, I was listening to Dr. Charles Stanley on the radio, and I knew in that moment this was the pastor and leader for my life to change. You can also experience this wonderful life-changing experience of transformation.

Dr. Charles Stanley - Sermon Notes – January 13, 2019 – WHEN GOD SPEAKS TO US – WE MUST COMPREHEND, CONFORM, AND COMMUNICATE AND THE CONDITION OF YOUR HEART

The church is just one way we are showing and telling God that He is worthy of our undivided attention. It is the perfect time for just you and God. God is always saying important things. God gets right to the point of things, and in many cases, is very direct and bold. When God speaks to us, we need to comprehend His message.

God will use these three words repeatedly to direct our lives: comprehend, conform, and communicate. Comprehend means "make it clear." God always speaks the truth. Dropping your guard and yielding to Him. There must be no resistance to God's will. Conform means "you are willing." God will deal with your whole life. He is in the process of shaping our lives for His likeness. Lastly, communicating means "you become bold about the truth of God and yourself." In some cases, this requires bold behavior to get the message across. There are two types of believers, according to Dr. Stanley, passive and aggressive.

The passive believer attends church sporadically, sometimes brings their Bible, may or may not enjoy the sermon, and misses God's message completely. The aggressive believer has the Bible in their hands, is eager to hear the sermon, is ready with a pen and notepad, listens carefully, is alert, and turns to select verses in the Bible. Aggressive believers listen to the mouth of God and not the mouth of Satan.

When we come to the House of the Lord, Dr. Stanley explains, we are asking God to give a listening heart. When God is speaking, God is worthy of our undivided attention. Mankind has little to say, but the Lord says it all. Remember, God is dealing with you directly, and He deserves your undivided attention. The wisest thing we can do is allow the truth to shape us in the mold of God. This may be a pleasant or unpleasant experience, but it is with God's love, for we do not walk in darkness but light.

THE CONDITION OF YOUR HEART

Living a lifestyle outside the will of God is very dangerous. When we do this, we are saying to God, "I don't' need you God, and my life seems to be going well." Satan will paint a picture so perfect just to get your attention, Dr. Stanley explains. However, Satan never reveals the outcome. By living Satan's ways, our behavior is out of sorts. Perhaps we are drinking too much, not attending church, or not studying the Word. Satan loves it when he separates the love of our children and parents, our finances go bad, our careers are destroyed, and we lose family and friends.

This is the true picture of Satan, who will blind your mind to the nature of sin and tell you that you feel good, look good, and will be just fine under his directions. All of these declarations are false. If you're wondering if Satan want to destroy you, ask yourself, "What is the condition of your heart?" God is always waiting to hear from us. When we feel lost, the first thing God says is, "I love you." God already knows you are unsatisfied with your current lifestyle. He also knows you can change it by changing the condition of your heart.

God loves you, and this is His wish for you.

**Dr. Charles Stanley – Sermon Notes – January
19, 2019 – THE CALL OF GOD**

Definition of Salvation – a saving or being saved, a person or thing that saves, a deliverance from sin and from the penalties of sin, redemption

Definition of Sanctification – to set apart as holy, consecrate, to make free from sin

Definition of Service – to do service for, aid, help, to meet the needs, to work as a servant, to carry out the duties of an office, as in order

Definition of Accountability – responsible, liable

Do you have a yearning or desire to hear God say to you, "Well done, good faithful servant?"

The call of God is very powerful. God did not create us to go through life alone. Through the Holy Spirit, God gives us the resources to lead us and provide help along the way. Please, do not miss the opportunity to respond to His call! There will be a day when we all must answer to God. It is important to note that God calls upon everyone; no one is left out. In His eyes, everyone is equally important.

"How do I know, I have received a command and or calling from God?" you may ask. Dr. Stanley would respond, "If you know who God is, you will know when He calls."

Please read Samuel 1: Samuel's Call, for it tells us that when we hear God's voice and His command, we are to respond, "Speak, Lord, for your servant is listening."

Dr. Stanley explains that the four important calls from God are salvation, sanctification, service, and accountability.

Call of Salvation — Have you been saved? Are you delivered from sin? Our Father is working daily in our lives. Allow God to come into your life and surrender your life to Him. Accept Him as your Lord Jesus Christ and your savior. Please make this your first priority.

Call of Sanctification — This is a specific call for holiness and cleansing. Evaluate your lifestyle. Do you represent God in His greatness? Are you living a lifestyle that is pleasing to God? Are you happy about the way you conduct yourself today, as well as the days after?

Call to Service — You are a child of God and His workmanship. God calls on each and every one of us to serve in different ways. God uses people like you and me. For example, if God knows you can handle a certain work in ministry, He indeed will use you for that. Call to Service – "God, this is not going to get done," you may say. "Please, do not hold me accountable." This is the attitude and voice of Satan, not God.

Call of Accountability — Do you adhere to the Ten Commandments? Do you use the gifts and talents He gave you? Do you help others in a time of need both spiritually and financially? Do you follow through on specific opportunities or do you throw them away? Do you love yourself and honor God in sobriety? Most importantly, do you love your neighbor as yourself?

Whatever acts you may or may not have done, God already knows them. Please, read, which tells us

> *But you, why do you criticize your brother? Or you, why do you look down on your brother? For we will all stand before the tribunal of God. For it is written: As I live, says the Lord, every knee will bow to Me, and every tongue will give praise to God.[e] So then, each of us will give an account of himself to God.*
> — Romans 14:10-12

This is God's warning of accountability. God wants to hear the truth!

If we love God, following through with His calling, ask God for His salvation, demonstrate our obedience to Him, in the end He will indeed say, "Well done, good faithful servant."

God loves you, and this is His wish for you.

3

Dr. Charles Stanley – Sermon Notes – January 20, 2019 – HOW DOES GOD GET YOUR ATTENTION?

1. Restless spirit — Yes, God will allow us to have a restless spirit. We all know when things are not going well, we just cannot pinpoint it. Losing sleep is usually the first indication something is wrong.
2. Someone else — Yes, God will go through someone else to get our attention. He has an open heart and will speak through others to get our undivided attention.
3. Unusual ways — Yes, God will use unusual ways to get our attention. He sees our plan in life. It is very clear with God if you are on a collision course, and if that's the case, He will use other methods. Our responsibility is to stop, look, and listen to what God is saying.
4. Unanswered prayers — Yes, God will use unanswered prayers to get our attention. This type of attention is not so pleasant. God is saying this is not My will for you, and He simply will close the door. His wish is that your re-exam yourself in the areas you need to deal with first. If God refuses your prayers, He may be saying, "You are not ready. You cannot handle this." However, God will use different methods until the right one works. God never gives up.
5. Disappointment — Yes, God will use disappointment. He may tell you it's all over or it's too late. God never gives up.

Be thankful and give praise to the One who knows you the best.

God loves you, and this is His wish for you.

**Dr. Charles Stanley – Sermon Notes – January 27, 2019 –
HOW DOES GOD GET OUR ATTENTION – Part 2**

Christ is our life and will allow unusual things to happen. Why? Because we are not listening to God when He speaks. God allows these unusual things to happen so He can get our attention. With God, there are no accidents. He is powerful in every situation. In some cases, we are not walking in the same Spirit of God, therefore, we tend to make plans that are not pleasing to Him, which can be the plans of Satan. We must learn to listen to God when He speaks.

Other methods of God are the loss of a job, the loss of one's finances, or even sickness. God may create a certain tragedy in your life. God's desire is for us to lean on Him at all times.

When God sends blessings, we are to act like it is Thanksgiving, and give God our undivided attention, praise God, and be so thankful for these blessings sent our way. God has His reasons why you have received these blessings.

As Christians, we must clean up our hearts first. Get right with God. Tell God you know you have made a foolish decision. When God is dealing with you, please do not get in His way. Be careful and don't challenge God, Dr. Stanley explains, for God knows exactly how to get your attention.

God loves you, and this is His wish for you.

Dr. Charles Stanley – Sermon Notes – February 3, 2019 – LISTENING TO GOD SPEAK

God's wish for us is that we convert to the likeliness of Jesus Christ to enhance our spiritual growth. Our spiritual growth is prayer and waiting for guidance. How do we know when God is speaking to us? Dr. Stanley warns about the different voices we hear, especially the one from Satan. The most important thing that Dr. Stanley mentions is the SIGNAL we need to pay attention to and the CALMNESS that enters our soul when we listen and recognize God's voice in prayer. When you feel total peace surrounding you and your heart and mind are at ease, this is God's voice speaking to you. The voice of Satan is one of destruction, where your heart and soul seem to be in havoc. You find yourself thinking in circles and your mind seems to be in overtime, not to mention you feel like you are swimming in mud. When this happens, erase Satan from your mind immediately and completely.

Other signals when we hear the voice of God:

1. Hearing God's voice is CONSISTENT. Focus on building scriptures into your mind. Remembering certain scriptures will allow us to help others, not just ourselves.
2. Hearing God's voice is not of CONFLICT. Is what you're hearing conflicting with God's teaching and counseling? Is this right or wrong? True believers will know instantly.
3. Hearing God's voice is CHALLENGING. Remember Dr. Stanley's lessons on "Testing and Temptations." Is this voice going to challenge my faith?

4. Hearing God's voice is COURAGE. Believing and trusting in God's promises. He sent His only Son, Jesus Christ, to die for our sins, and He was risen in three days.
5. Hearing God's voice CLASH. Other voices just don't make any sense at all.
6. Hearing God's voice is CALMNESS. This is the most important signal. God loves you and will calm you in every situation. Calmness brings, love, peace, joy, happiness, and the ability to think clearly and wisely.

Jesus Christ experienced all these voices in order for Him to become a great teacher and counselor to mankind. When receiving advice from other people, Dr. Stanley suggests being respectful but remember to always check out their lifestyle. If their advice does not feel or set right, it probably is not good advice. Always turn to God FIRST for advice.

Televised – Sermon Notes – Dr. Charles Stanley – February 3, 2019

LIVING A LIFE THAT COUNTS:

You cannot escape the opportunity to be somebody from God. Why? You are the Light of the World.

The world has a different message for you other than the message from God, which is living eternal life in heaven with Him forever. We all know the message the world sends out — living the life of a nonbeliever and living a life in the fast lane.

> *I will instruct you and show you the way to go; with My eye on you, I will give counsel. Do not be like a horse or mule, without understanding, that must be controlled with bit and bridle or else it will not come near you.*

Many pains come to the wicked, but the one who trusts in the Lord will have faithful love surrounding him. Be glad in the Lord and rejoice you righteous ones; shout for joy, all you upright in heart.

— Psalms 32:8-11

Let the light shine through…daily we are to be reflectors of light so others may see our goodwill. We are all reflectors in some way through the eyes of God.

— Matthew 5:16

Dr. Stanley says we maybe a birthday candle or a huge beam, but somehow, we all matter in the eyes of God.

"Like it or not, that is the way it is," he explains. No escaping.

God loves you, and this is His wish for you.

6

Dr. Charles Stanley – Sermon Notes – February 17, 2019
LISTENING TO GOD AND OUR VIEWPOINT OF GOD

How do we know we are listening to God in the right way? First, we must know what our relationship is with God. Here are the questions you need to ask yourself:

Ask yourself, what is my attitude like? God will instruct you to be submissive.

Ask yourself, how well do I trust God? God will show guidance. It's our responsibility to trust and believe in God. He will never point you in the wrong direction.

Ask yourself, how thankful are you? So thankful that if you were born with no father figure, God gave you a substitute? So thankful for teachers and counselors to help those with no father authority? These are the blessings that God promised, and it is our responsibility to act accordingly.

Everyone needs a counselor at some point in their life, Dr. Stanley tells us. Interesting to note, when you do hear God speak, He will be speaking the truth, therefore, we must listen and be tentative. God's intent for you is not destruction but one of glory. Glory, that you may spend eternal life with Him in heaven forever and ever — if your relationship is right, if your attitude of God is right, if your trust is right, and if your thankfulness is right. However, you must be obeying God's Rules of the Law – the Bible — Dr. Stanley says.

Dr. Charles Stanley – televised sermon – February 17, 2019

THE MODERN DAY SAMARITAN:

In Luke 10:25-29, The Parable of the Good Samaritan, one man asked God, "What do I need to do to inherit eternal life?" This story is about three men who one day approached a beaten man on the streets. Two of the men passed him by, but the third stop to offer help. This seems like a very simple story, but this message by far is not simple. God will evaluate your heart and not your works. Yes, it is your service to mankind that counts.

What is a good Samaritan?

Open Eyes – Observe any situation in a compassionate way. This maybe the perfect calling; to witness to that hurting person. Please, do not miss out.

Open Heart — Open your heart with compassion. When this happens, is your heart beating faster and faster in blood or faster and faster in spiritual compassion?

Open Hands — Extend your hand with a firm honest handshake.

Open Possessions — We have already received so many blessings from God, but think about the person who has not. They have nothing. Our possessions have come from God, so they're really God's possessions and not ours. There are the people who desperately need a blessing.

Open Time — This is very difficult in the busy world we live in. Ask yourself, "Did I make the right decision? Did I listen to the heart God gave me?"

Have you ever loved someone to the point you can feel their pain?
A good samaritan can.

Are you a good Samaritan?

God loves you, and this is His wish for you.

7

Dr. Charles Stanley – Sermon Notes – February 24, 2019 – LISTENING WHEN GOD SPEAKS

When God speaks to us, we should be actively listening. In order for us to hear from God, we must spend time in prayer or meditation. This is a quiet time for you and God to speak to each other. As quoted in 1 Samuel 3:10, "Speak, for thy servant is listening to God." We are God's servant, and it's our responsibility to listen carefully to what God has to say. Dr. Stanley tells us God always speaks the truth. Listening is not passive, but active, when God speaks.

IMPORTANT CATEGORIES OF FAITH THAT WE MUST LEARN AND UNDERSTAND:

EXPECTING – This is likely to occur or appear. When God speaks to me or calls on me, I will actively answer.

QUIETLY – not noisy or speaking, but stillness and calmness. I will be still and know I'm listening to God speak.

PATIENTLY – God will only tell us certain things, or He may withhold information, because we are not ready. This is an active way God is reaching and or stretching our faith. God is drawing you near to Him before He honors your request.

ACTIVELY – We must actively spend time in the Word of God for us to hear from God.

CONFIDENTLY – I will hear what I want to hear from God.

HUMBLY — God already knows our shortcomings, and He wants us to know them too. Lower yourself in pride and be humble. Be in recognition of the Holy Spirit for the truth. Ask yourself, "Do I have the right relationship with God? Am I walking in the ways of God?" Listen to the Holy Spirit and know your relationship with God. Two very important things: by faith we are to listen when God speaks and not rebellion against God. The Holy Spirit cannot deliver, because you cannot hear God, Dr. Stanley says. This is what happens when we do not listen. Be aware that believers and or Christians can be in total error by not listening when God speaks.

OPENLY – Be free to speak to God honestly. God does not discriminate or hold things against you to punish you. Our God loves you and is our protector. Our requests or prosperity should fit in God's plan, not our own. God always knows what is best.

ATTENTIVELY – Pay attention and be devoted to God at all times. He will use others to speak to us, but we must always check to see if God's fingerprint is there. Always go to God first, "Is this right or wrong?"

CAREFULLY – Is what we hear a contradiction to the Word of God? Know that God is our one and only judge of what is really happening. God knows our situation, so let Him deal with all circumstances. If it's not from God, then you must throw it out. Whatever we hear must be verified in the Bible. It must be consistent with the scriptures and feed your spiritual life with the Word of God, Dr. Stanley explains.

SUBMISSIVELY – This is the perfect time to offer an opinion – to yield.

GRATEFULLY – "For God so loved the world he gave is one and only Son to die on the cross for our sins," John 3:16 tells us. We are now a Child of God and should show thanksgiving in all that we do.

REVERING — Appreciate God's love and deep respect. God created us with an amazing capacity. He named all the stars in the galaxy and all the fish in the ocean. He created the whole universe and everything in it.

Just listen. That's how much God loves you and me.

8

Dr. Charles Stanley – Sermon Notes – March 7, 2019 – HUNGER AND THIRST

Do you have a lukewarm or serious relationship with God?

You may say to yourself, "No one understands me." Oh, but God does!

Philippians 4:7 says, "And the peace of God, which surpasses every thought, will guard your hearts and your minds in Christ Jesus."

Is your hunger and thirst for something or somebody? Dr. Stanley says if we are not in a relationship with our Lord Jesus Christ, we are missing the very best. Therefore, we must seek a personal relationship with God, making this the first priority in our life.

Is your relationship with our Heavenly Father lukewarm or serious? Are you wrapped up in worldly things? Stop and get wrapped up in God, Dr. Stanley proclaims. Thoughts that are appealing to the flesh and or for gratification, as well as sin, are what Dr. Stanley is referring to.

How do you know if I have a personal relationship with God? The answer is when you ask Jesus Christ to come into your life as your personal savior. Once you have completed this, your hunger and thirst for God will increase daily — you just simply can't get enough!

Here are three helpful steps to achieving hunger and thirst that are serious:

1. Study the Bible and learn how God thinks. Mediate and listen when God speaks; let God do all the talking. If you can't keep quiet and have a desire in your heart to share with others, dig deeper in the Word. It is like digging for gold, build your faith in the person of God, pursing the Will of God. Your faith will grow principle after principle.

2. Do you love to spend time with God? He says, "I'm a body with you. I want to spend time with you. What are you praying for?" Do you thank God instead of asking for things? The Bible applies to all of us. Do you request God's answers in the right way? As adults, we don't have to beg from God. We learn to trust instead and learn to understand who God is.

3. God always saves the best for last — you are set free. With all the tug and pull from the World, God will satisfy you, and in return, your freedom will be restored. When God is the number one priority in your life, every emotion you have will be turned over to God, and He will take over from there. Dr. Stanley says it is a mystery how this happens, but when we trust and obey, all our hunger and thirst are directed towards a serious relationship with God. God loves you, and this is His wish for you.

Dr. Charles Stanley – Sermon Notes – March 10, 2019 – PRAY WITH CONFIDENCE

There are times in our life we may wonder why God delays answering our prayers. Prayer is not easy. It is very important that we understand why God sometimes delays, Dr. Stanley says. God will check our confidence in prayer, and He will act if your prayer glorifies Him. This is very normal, and God understands that sometimes we may become impatient and even get angry. Dr. Stanley reminds us to set aside our impatientence, keep praying, and don't give up.

Please read Matthew 7:7, which tells us, "Ask and it will be given to you, seek and you will find; knock and the door will be opened to you. For everyone who asks receives; he who seeks finds; and to him who knocks, the door will be opened."

When we practice "prayer with confidence," we discover the Will of God. Dr. Stanley explains, real genuine prayer is hard work, and at times, it is so overwhelming, you just simply want to give up. This may be a challenge from God to see how we react. When we acknowledge that He is in control of all things, God has all the power and perfect wisdom. This becomes our genuine way to think and react. God takes a personal interest in everyone's life and has a higher purpose for prayer. Realize that God is in control of everything, and our job is to pray with confidence. Trust in our Heavenly Father, who loves us.

When we don't pray the right way, Dr. Stanley calls this "weak prayer life." We must change this habit and attitude. First, build an intimate personal relationship with God. This means to OPEN UP, TRUST, BELIEVE, FORGIVE AND BE HONEST. This is the beginning to building a personal relationship! Secondly, we acknowledge God is the source of all things, and God wants us to depend upon Him. We must view God for who He is — loving, kind, and caring, His plan for our life is a great one. BE CONFIDENT, and view God for who He is, Our Heavenly Father. Start your prayers with, "Our Heavenly Father." God wants us to learn His ways and how He operates. God promises to work it out.

Learn and practice waiting. Trust in God for all things, for we must wait upon Him. God has the right timing. We must learn to trust and wait. When we obey God in these commands, the non-believers will observe our actions. Get their attention, and the non-believer will become a believer in our Lord Jesus Christ. It's a miracle!

How does a person realize that God is his Father? God sees our hopelessness. He will remind us of the significance of our Lord Jesus Christ, Son of God, the person who died on the cross and paid the price for all our sins.

Please read 1 John: The Word Became Flesh.

God loves you, and this is His wish for you.

Dr. Charles Stanley – Sermon Notes March 17, 2019 – PRAY WITH CONFIDENCE – Part 2

God does not cater to our schedule; therefore we must have patience and wait for God to answer prayers. Dr. Stanley asks the question, "Do you have the right to ask for something?" The answer is absolutely, it's fine to ask God. In fact, it is pleasing to Him. God considers this a privilege and desires to demonstrate and honor your prayer. That's how much God loves us.

God enjoys answering prayers. God keeps His promises.

Building confidence with God. What happens if you're asking for the wrong thing, and God doesn't answer your prayer request? If your prayer does not fit the Will of God, it's because God has something better for you. God does not dish out prayer answers if you ignore Him and His Will. It's important to check your prayer life with God. Is it a poor prayer life?

Here are the reasons God may delay answering prayers. Is there sin in your life? Are you manipulating your own circumstances and/or making your own arrangements and plans? God may also delay answering prayers, because the timing is not right. God may be testing your faith and patience. Is your faith genuine? Can you look beyond your circumstances and turn everything over to God? God wants to demonstrate His plan for your life. When you experience heartache, pain, and sorrow in life, these emotions come from God. Once you obey and become strengthened in the Word, these emotions will turn into peace, love, and joy because it's the Will of God and His plan for your life. You must first learn to walk right with God.

We must learn to listen when God speaks, Dr. Stanley explains. God does all the talking, and we are to listen. Unfortunately, some people never reach their maximum potential when speaking to God. Dr. Stanley tells us we should be quiet and let God do all the speaking. God has a desire to speak directly to your heart. Our responsibility is to trust, obey, and believe in our Heavenly Father and listen.

The smartest thing we can do today is get down on your knees and just listen to God speak. Open your heart, mind, and spirit and listen. God will keep His promise and answer your prayers in His time.

God loves you, and this is His wish for you.

Dr. Charles Stanley – Sermon Notes – March 24, 2019 – HUNGER AND THIRST FOR GOD

Definition of Hunger – a desire

Definition of Thirst – a strong desire or craving

Please remember that God is the center of our life all day long.

What are you holding on to? What satisfies you? What satisfies your Spirit?

> *As a deer longs for streams of water, so I long for You, God. I thirst for God, the living God. When can I come and appear before God? My tears have been my food day and night, while all day long people say to me, "Where is your God?"*
> — Psalms 42:1-3

This scripture is as an example, of a deer craving for water, which is like our craving to have more of our Lord Jesus Christ. This is the right way to think and believe, which holds the key to a successful relationship with God and brings peace, joy, contentment, and love into our life. This is our Christian maturity, Dr. Stanley explains.

How strong is your desire to have God in your heart? Christians must examine their hearts. Is it lukewarm? Do you crave God's presence daily? Your goal is to develop a deeper and deeper personal relationship with our Lord Jesus Christ. Living in the world today, Dr. Stanley says, there is a lot of competition out there. Don't let Satan destroy your work in progress with God. Satan's desire is to attack. It is so important to develop Christian maturity and stop Satan.

As early as birth, God placed hunger and thirst in each child regardless of their environment. He also created two types of parents, those who instilled God into their lives and parents who did not. God instructs us to Honor thy Father and Mother. So, from the very beginning of our life, we have always had hunger and thirst for God. God has always been aware of our relationship with Him. When we experience difficult times, it is God who all along is drawing us back-back to Him. Yes, when we stray, God knows and is always willing to love us, forgive us, and welcome us back to Him with loving arms. God is so powerful that just knowing this should make us feel like dropping to our knees in prayer and thanksgiving.

Once you have fulfilled your hunger and thirst for God, Dr. Stanley explains, you will have blessings of happiness, contentment, joy, peace, and love. There is no competition with God.

Do you wish for a hotdog or a piece of beef? Only you can answer this question. Why? Because God is drawing you more and more to Him to satisfy your hunger and thirst. It is through your renewed relationship with Him. True Christian maturity is craving more and more for our Lord Jesus Christ.

God loves you, and this is His wish for you.

**Dr. Charles Stanley – Sermon Notes – April 14, 2019
– GOD'S PLAN FOR OUR RESURRECTION**

If we are wise, we will read scriptures and learn the importance of the Resurrection of Jesus and how it affects each and every one of us. Dr. Stanley asks that we don't ignore the Resurrection. I have never felt comfortable or qualified to write on the topics of the Crucifixtion and the Resurrection. The thought process is deep in detail, and the message has to be clear and perfect. However, I do understand that when our almighty Jesus Christ died, God used His death as an example of what our death will be if you are a believer in our Lord Jesus Christ. Dr. Stanley focuses on St. Paul's writings in 1 Corinthians 15. I also realize that God is the authority, captain and general over everything. God created us, and He knew that we would fail and be sinful. Perhaps call this a test or temptation of His love for us.

I suggest you read 1 Corinthians 15, which is the Resurrection Essential to the Gospel, Resurrection Essential to the Faith, Christ's Resurrection Guarantees Ours, Resurrection Supported by Christian Experience, The Nature of the Resurrection Body, and Victorious Resurrection.

> *But now Christ has been raised from the dead, the firstfruits of those who have fallen asleep. For since death came through a man, the resurrection of the dead also comes through a man.*
>
> – 1 Corinthians 15:20-21

There is no right time in our life to ask God to come into our lives. The Easter holiday is a great time to surrender to God, tell God you believe that He sent His only Son Jesus Christ to die on the cross and pay for our sins, and ask forgiveness for yours. When you accept Our Lord Jesus Christ as your Savior, God will open His arms to you, and you will immediately become a child of God. With God, there are no questions asked. Why? Because He created you, and He already knows your circumstances. God's wish is that you believe, love one another, and walk in His ways.

God loves you, and this is His wish for you.

Dr. Charles Stanley – Sermon Notes – Easter Sunday – April 21, 2019 – GOD'S PLAN FOR OUR RESURRECTION

On Easter Sunday, we celebrate Our Lord Jesus Christ risen from the grave, the perfect Son of God who was crucified on the Cross at Calvary. We have so many reasons to rejoice, and they are plentiful. Psalm 103, The Forgiving God, explains God's plan for our resurrection.

How do we know we are a child of God?

> *But to all who did receive Him, He gave them the right to be children of God, to those who believe in His name, who were born, not of blood, or of the will of the flesh, or of the will of man, but of God.*
>
> John 1:12-13

How do we know the story of Jesus is true?

There are two reasons — the empty tomb and the eyewitness. If you're in need of clarification, then I suggest you look at:

- Matthew 27:45 - The Death of Jesus
- Matthew 27:57 – The Burial of Jesus
- Matthew 27:62 – The Closely Guarded Tomb
- Mathew 28:1 – Resurrection Morning
- Matthew 28:11 – The Soldiers Bribed to Lie

How may we look at death?

But now Christ has been raised from the dead, the first fruits of those who have fallen asleep. 21 For since death came through a man, the resurrection of the dead also comes through a man. 22 For just as in Adam all die, so also in Christ all will be made alive.

— 1 Corinthians 15:20-22

When Jesus was talking with His friend Martha right before His death, He said to her, "I am the resurrection and the life. The one who believes in me, even if he dies, will live. Everyone who lives and believes in me will never die. Do you believe this?" Martha replied, "Yes, Lord, I believe you are the Messiah, the Son of God, who comes into the world."

God loves you, and this is His wish for you.

14

Dr. Charles Stanley – Sermon Notes – April 28, 2019 –
TURNING DOUBTS INTO BLESSED ASSURANCE

Definition of Salvation: a saving or being saved; a person or thing that saves; deliverance from sin and from the penalties of sin; redemption.

Definition of Baptism: the sacrament of admitting a person into a Christian church by immersing the individual in water or by sprinkling water on the individual; an initiating experience.

How do you know my saalvation with the Lord Jesus Christ is right? How do you really know that you're saved? When you walked down a church-isle as a child, is that when you were saved? You may think, "I don't remember anything about being dunked, dipped, or have someone sprinkle water over me." Be very sensitive to people when you talk to them about their Salvation. Satan will harass and try to block your Salvation and love for our Lord Jesus Christ. Please, don't let this happen.

First, start by asking yourself these questions: Have I confessed that Jesus Christ is our LORD and that God raised him from the dead? Second, have you been baptized? When we become baptized, this is a public announcement that we now have a private relationship with Jesus Christ. We are letting others witness this awesome celebration of becoming a child of God. It's a happy day where you celebrate your new life as a Christian and share it with others. Don't rebel against baptism. It is highly important, as it represents where you will be spending your eternal life. You MUST be baptized. In the Bible, before Jesus died, He instructed

His disciples to go into all nations to teach and to baptize. Jesus does not care about your past, and you don't have to live a perfect life, but you MUST believe in Him and be baptized. This is when you decide where you will spend your eternal life — in Heaven or a lake of fire.

> *I assure you: Anyone who hears My word and believes Him who sent Me has eternal life and will not come under judgment but has passed from death to life. I assure you: An hour is coming, and is now here, when the dead will hear the voice of the Son of God, and those who hear will live.*
>
> — John 5:24-25

There are reasons we may doubt our blessed assurance of salvation. — sin, questions of your self esteem, false teaching, changing emotions, (don't allow your emotions to overcome you), ignorance (i.e. no one ever taught or told me), and comparing yourself with other people. Furthermore, certain trials and circumstance, such as asking God, "Why did you allow this to happen?" These are all things that can raise doubt and warrant our caution and attention.

God loves you, and this is His wish for you.

Dr. Charles Stanley - Sermon Notes - May 5, 2019 - TURNING DOUBTS INTO BLESSED ASSURANCE – Part 2

Definition of Salvation: a saving or being saved; a person or thing that saves; deliverance from sin and from the penalties of sin; redemption.

Ask yourself this question today, "Do I feel that I'm saved?" Dr. Stanley tells us we have categories of knowing if we are saved or not:

1. You immediately know if you are saved or not.
2. You think you are saved but are not sure.
3. You are not a believer.
4. You desire salvation.

I believe what Dr. Stanley is trying to explain is that you need to clear things up inside ourselves. In order for us to turn doubts into blessed assurance, you need to get busy and know what your relationship is with Jesus now. Let pondering days be gone, and make this decision as soon as possible. How do you do that? It's an inner spiritual gift from God, our Heavenly Father. Start by saying a private prayer, and tell God you are ready to surrender your life, confess your sins, and you believe that Jesus Christ is the Son of God, who paid the price for all our sins so that we may have eternal life. Once you make this decision, you are a Child of God, allowing peace to come into your life. Past doubts you once had are now turned into blessed assurance.

You know now that you're a born again Christian and where you want to spend eternity. You understand how God works in the human heart, and He has changed your life forever. You're a believer and want to stay in the word. Thankfully, you have cleared up things in your relationship with Jesus Christ. It's not God's way to complicate matters. He is a loving God and will keep His promise, because He knows what is best.

> *For this is the will of My Father: that everyone who sees the Son and believes in Him may have eternal life, and I will raise him up on the last day."*
> — John 6:40

God's desire, is that no one will be cast out. This is God's gift to us. Do not ignore this most precious opportunity to spend eternity with our Heavenly Father.

God loves you, and this is His wish for you.

Dr. Charles Stanley – Sermon Notes - May 12, 2019 – LETTING GO OF ANGER

Definition of Anger — a feeling of displeasure and hostility that a person has because of being injured, mistreated, opposed; to make angry.

How do you know if you are angry or not? If anger is in your heart, then it is "working anger," Dr. Stanley says, however if you are a believer, you do not need to live with anger. Anger is dangerous, and affects you mentally, physically, and emotionally. It can destroy relationships, marriages, and careers. Dr. Stanley tells us there are two kinds of anger — justified and unjustified. Justified anger is fair, using authority to uphold what is just. Unjustified anger is where you witness unfairness, such as something that might have happened to you personally or perhaps something unjust happened to a family member.

Don't surround yourself with angry people, Dr. Stanley warns. When this happens, their anger becomes yours. It's important to enter marriage when both parties have openly discussed their healthy and unhealthy anger. It's also important to look at their family. Living with anger is unhealthy.

Dr. Stanley compared a pressure cooker to anger as an example. Anger inside of you just keeps boiling and building up to the point it explodes. No one wants that anger, which is why we must be slow to anger (good or bad) and ask forgiveness. Pray and identify what you are angry about and ask forgiveness, pray that your attitude will be transformed to be justified and pleasing. Pray that your anger will be disposed of. Pray that you will have the confidence and discipline to walk in the ways of our Heavenly Father so that you may experience eternity and not the lake of fire.

There is only one way we, as human beings, can deal with anger — by the Grace of God. If you have an anger problem, admit it, and ask forgiveness, even if you have been wronged. Satan loves to see angry people, because when you get mad and or angry, it takes away the love that you have for our Heavenly Father, and gives that love to Satan.

> *Since you put away lying, Speak the truth, each one to his neighbor, because we are members of one another. Be angry and do not sin. Don't let the sun go down on your anger, and don't give the Devil an opportunity.*
> — Ephesians 4:25-27

> *A gentle answer turns away anger, but a harsh word stirs up wrath.*
> — Proverbs 15:1

Be slow to anger. Are you an angry person? If so, ask forgiveness and ask God to transform your life to stop this unnecessary anger. Be honest with God, and tell Him you know this anger inside is taking time away from Him.

God loves you, and this is His wish for you.

Dr. Charles Stanley Sermon Notes - May 26, 2019 - LETTING GO OF ANGER - Part 2

Definition of Anger – distress; a feeling of displeasure and hostility that a person has because of being injured, mistreated, or opposed.

Anger is natural and normal, Dr. Stanley explains, and are suggestions from him on how to deal with it. A person would be wise to practice these techniques and deal with anger in the correct way.

Have you ever blamed someone else for your anger? Dr. Stanley told the story of a woman who approached him one day and said, "I'm angry at you. No, I'm not angry at you, but I'm angry at God." Shortly after, she corrected it to, "No, I'm angry at myself."

This is how mixed up you can get when you do not identify anger in the correct way. You must identify your anger properly to respond properly. Do not harbor your anger. There are some people are still angry at loved ones who have passed on, Dr. Stanley mentions.

We all have the capacity for anger, so what are you going to do about your anger? How do you respond properly when you get angry?

> *No rotten talk should come from your mouth, but only what is good for the building up of someone in need, to give grace to those who hear. 30 And don't grieve God's Holy Spirit, who sealed you for the day of redemption. 31 All bitterness, anger and wrath, insult and slander*

must be removed from you, along with all wickedness.
32 And be kind and compassionate to one another,
forgiving one another, just as God also forgave you in
Christ.

– Ephesians 4:29-32

God addresses anger: 1) we repress, hold back and deny our anger, 2) anger can be seen in a person's eyes and voice; your eyes cannot hide anger, 3) go into outburst, our anger just keeps getting deeper, 4) we have excuses for anger, there is some type of short-fuse, 5) we choose to be angry, 6) listen to the Holy Spirit and allow God to respond for you.

Here are some suggestions from Dr. Stanley on how to handle your anger:

- build up a defense mechanism, and don't respond in the incorrect way
- confess your anger, and examine the poison inside of you that makes you angry
- identify the source of your anger, such as where it started and by whom
- deal with your anger immediately

Stop, listen, and take a timeout before responding to anger. Let your accuser do all the speaking while you quietly listen. If it is unjust, you probably won't be able to think clearly nor respond in the correct way. This is normal, so the best thing to do is be patient and listen. When you do speak, ask the other person if there is anything else they wish to share. Usually, this will stop that person from being angry with you.

The Lord is compassionate and gracious, slow to anger and full of faithful love. 9 He will not always accuse [us] or be angry forever.

— Psalms 103-8-9

My dearly loved brothers, understand this: everyone must be quick to hear, slow to speak, and slow to anger, 20 for man's anger does not accomplish God's righteousness.

— James 1:19-20

The Bible is so accurate, and God makes no mistakes.

God loves you, and this is His wish for you.

18

Dr. Charles Stanley – June 9, 2019 – Sermon Notes – LETTING GO OF ANGER – Part 3

Definition of Anger – a feeling of displeasure and hostility that a person has because of being injured, mistreated, opposed

Definition of Hostility – a feeling of enmity, ill will; an expression of enmity, ill will, warfare

Definition of Enmity – the bitter attitude or feelings of an enemy or enemies; hostility

Definition of Bitterness - causing or showing sorrow, pain, sharp and disagreeable; harsh, resentful, or cynical

Definition of Fool – a silly or stupid person; a victim of a trick, dupe; to act like a fool; to joke

Definition of Betrayal – to fail to uphold; to betray a trust; to deceive; to seduce and then desert; to reveal unknowingly; to disclose a secret

We must learn to forgive others to have a personal relationship with God. Our connection with Him is so critical, because we want to obey, live a Godly life, and spend eternity in Heaven instead of the Lake of Fire. It's not easy to forgive someone who hurt or betrayed you. However, it's a requirement from God. WE MUST FORGIVE.

How do you learn to forgive someone? *Pray.*

Therefore, you should pray like this: Our Father in heaven, your name be honored as holy. Your kingdom comes. Your will be done on earth as it is in heaven. Give us today our daily bread. And forgive us our debts, as we also have forgiven our debtors. And do not bring us into temptation but deliver us from the evil one. [For Yours is the kingdom and the power and the glory forever. Amen.} For if you forgive people their wrongdoing, your heavenly Father will forgive you as well. But if you don't forgive people, your Father will not forgive your wrongdoing.

– Matthew 6:9-15

Definition of Forgive – to give up resentment against or the desire to punish.

Definition of Unforgiving – not willing or not able to forgive

Where do you want to spend eternity?

To forgive is an eternity in Heaven; to not forgive is an eternity in the Lake of Fire?

God loves you, and this is His wish for you.

19

Dr. Charles Stanley – Sermon Notes – June 2, 2019 – LETTING GO OF ANGER - HOW TO HANDLE ANGER

Definition of Anger – a feeling of displeasure and hostility that a person has because of being injured, mistreated, oppressed

Definition of Hostility – a feeling of enmity, ill will; an expression of enmity, ill will, warfare

Definition of Enmity – the bitter attitude or feelings of an enemy or enemies; hostility

Definition of Vent – expression; release; (giving vent to emotion) let it out

Definition of Bitterness – causing or showing sorrow, pain, sharp and disagreeable; harsh, resentful, or cynical

Definition of Fool – a silly or stupid person; a victim of a trick; duped; to act like a fool; to joke

Did you know that living with anger is also living with bitterness? Dr. Stanley tells us bitterness is not pretty, it is ugly. However, you must deal with anger and bitterness. How can you set yourself free from these two very strong emotions?

Start by building up a defense mechanism, confess you have built up anger, and don't repress your anger. Next, clarify and analyze what is creating this anger. For example, is this person angry themselves? Do they seem to be frustrated with their life? Do they feel insecure about something or someone? Are they jealous people? Then, deal with the problem, which is called a vent (get it out). Don't turn into a lion, tiger, or bear. Out of respect, we must learn to listen first and respond at the proper time. It's very necessary to confront this emotion of anger by handling anger right away.

Don't be labeled a "fool" with anger. How do you do that? This is where you choose to not allow anger inside you. Simply refuse to allow anger inside your heart and soul. Get rid of anger that controls you. You can use helpful tools like washing and waxing your car, cleaning out your closets, or go workout at the gym. Don't blow up, instead, turn negative anger into positive anger. This is where you turn the corner on anger.

THE RIGHT WAY TO HANDLE ANGER

Go somewhere alone, such as your car (don't drive), bathroom, or bedroom. Get on your knees and pray. Ask God to forgive your anger and bitterness. Get it all out with God. The anger you are holding inside is now with God (let go and let God). God already knows the anger you are experiencing. Why does God allow this anger to happen? It's God's way of telling you to turn your anger over to Him. God is drawing you nearer to him. That's how much God loves us. He carries everyone's anger. What a blessing this is. Did you know your help with anger is already waiting for you when you turn it over to God?

> *And don't grieve God's Holy Spirit, who sealed you for the day of redemption. All bitterness, anger and wrath, insult and slander must be removed from you, along with all wickedness. And be kind and compassionate to one another, forgiving one another, just as God also forgave you in Christ.*
>
> — Ephesians 4:30-32

Therefore, God's chosen ones, holy and loved, put on heartfelt compassion, kindness, humility, gentleness, and patience, accepting one another and forgiving one another if anyone has a complaint against another. Just as the Lord has forgiven you, so also you must [forgive]. Above all, [put on] love-the perfect bond of unity.
— Colossians 3:12-14

Are there benefits of anger? Yes, Dr. Stanley explains, you can learn to deal with your anger and bitterness. Anger is a motivator. You can get up and do something about anger, such as making something positive happen. Now that we know how to analyze properly, we can also prevent anger from reoccurring by utilizing our special "anger tools." It's important to stay away from angry people. Do not marry a person prone to anger because their anger becomes your anger.

Lastly, don't shut out God from your anger and bitterness. God loves and cares for you very much. He is illustrating to you how to become a "perfect disciple" by becoming responsible and conducting and adjusting your behavior to be pleasing to Him. It's your responsibility to trust in God when it comes to your anger and bitterness.

God loves you, and this is His wish for you.

**Dr. Charles Stanley – Sermon Notes –
June 16, 2019 - FATHER'S DAY
LETTING GO OF ANGER – Part 4**

Did you know having an unforgiving attitude toward anger is a violation of God? He will change your attitude towards anger and has the awesome power to do so. God has the power of forgiveness. To stop anger, something must change first.

How do you deal with anger? First, you must identify the anger inside. God is aware of how you have been treated by someone. Deep down inside, this anger has been building up. So, you must forgive FIRST. When you forgive FIRST, you set other people free. Second, go to that person. Here is what you say to them:

1. Acknowledge to them you have had an ungodly attitude towards them, and now with the help of the Holy Spirit, you ask for their forgiveness. Be free to say whatever is on your mind. You forgive FIRST. You no longer want to be a slave to anger.
2. Confess your rage and anger towards them.
3. Realize unforgiveness is a violation of God.
4. Confess you have asked God to forgive you, for what you said or did was wrong. Through the act of my will, and the power of the Holy Spirit, I lay down this terrible anger.
5. Ask them to forgive you.
6. Lastly, tell them you have chosen to lay down this anger, and that is the end of it.

Forgiving does not come instantly, it takes time. Dr. Stanley encourages you to practice your conversation by getting a chair and pretending you are talking to that individual. Practice it repeatedly.

Go to prayer.

Dear Heavenly Father, thank you for my forgiveness from anger. Thank you for healing my heart from slavery to anger. Tell God how this has changed your attitude and life. Confess to God you are a better person for asking forgiveness FIRST. Tell God you now are wise enough and have the courage to let Him set you free. Tell God you now realize a free man is different than an enslaved man.

Your goal is freedom in your life from anger. We must forgive and forgive first.

God loves you, and this is His wish for you.

21

Dr. Charles Stanley – Sermon Notes – June 23, 2019 – BY THE GRACE OF GOD

Definition of Grace – the love and favor toward human beings

Grace is a pure gift to us from God. "Grace to you, grace is with you," are words of importance. However, we must have a clear understanding of the word Grace, and what it means when we hear the word.

What does it mean to you when you hear the word "God?" Do you think about Father, Judge, guilt, sinfulness, fear, rejection, emptiness, or love? It's important to note these words, and the thoughts you have are very normal when you think about our Lord.

Grace is not about your work, nor is it about the quality of work. We may talk about our work, but we forget our sinfulness. In addition, you cannot purchase grace. It is unearned and undeserved. God's plan is for us to live in humility. Our humility draws us near to Him. Yes, God wants us to always depend upon Him. He uses humility to seek His desire, so that we may be wise enough to live by the grace of God.

> *Likewise, you younger men, be subject to the elders. And all of you clothe yourselves with humility toward one another, because God resists the proud, but gives grace to the humble. 6 Humble yourselves therefore under the mighty hand of God, so that He may exalt you in due time, 7 casting all your care upon Him, because He cares about you.*
> – 1 Peter 5:5-7

What do we do about Grace? In the scriptures, here is what God does about His grace:

> *Now if by grace, then it is not by works; otherwise, grace ceases to be grace.*
>
> — Romans 11:6

You are saved by the grace of God. It's unearned and undeserved but by our Heavenly Father. God reminds us that Jesus Christ paid our sins in full by His death at Calvary as the perfect Grace of God.

> *For we do not have a high priest who is unable to sympathize with our weaknesses, but one who has been tested in every way as we are, yet without sin. Therefore, let us approach the throne of grace with boldness, so that we may receive mercy and find grace to help us at the proper time.*
>
> — Hebrew 4:15-16

Lastly, set aside all your pride and boastfulness. It is harmful and turns away from God.

God loves you, and this is His wish for you.

Dr. Charles Stanley – Sermon Notes – June 30, 2019 – OUR GOD OF GRACE

Definition of Grace – the love and favor toward human beings

Definition of Mercy – a disposition to forgive or be kind; the power to forgive; a refraining from harming offenders, enemies

By accepting the Lord Jesus Christ as your savior, you are accepting God's awesome gift of grace. There is no other way to spend eternal life in Heaven. The goodness, love and kindness of God are by His grace and His love for all mankind.

Grace is undeserved and unearned. The only way we can live by grace is to accept the Lord Jesus Christ as our savior. Dr. Stanley teaches that Jesus lived a perfect life with no sin, and we too must demonstrate this character. The greatest gift of grace was God sacrificing His only Son.

> *For all have sinned and fall short of the glory of God. They are justified freely by His grace through the redemption that is in Christ Jesus.*
> *— Romans 3:23-24*

God is aware of our helplessness, which is why He chose his perfect Son to die on the cross for all humanity. Please do not reject the gift of grace to you from God.

> *But God, who is abundant in mercy, because of His great love that He had for us, 5 made us alive with the*

Messiah even though we were dead in trespasses. By grace you are saved!

— Ephesians 2:4-5

When we accept the Lord Jesus Christ as our savior, we experience the new birth and a new life. It is the only way to spend eternity with our Heavenly Father.

God's awesome gift of grace is to accept Him as our savior.

God loves you, and this is His wish for you.

Dr. Charles Stanley – Sermon Notes – July 7, 2019 – GRACE ON DISPLAY

Definition of Grace — the love and favor of God toward all human beings

Definition of Blasphemer – to speak evil; to speak profanely of or to (God or sacred things) to curse

Definition of Persecutor – to afflict constantly to injure or distress, as for reasons of religion, race

Definition of Arrogant – to claim, full of or due to pride; haughty

Definition of Haughty – having or showing great pride in oneself and contempt for others

Definition of Surrender – to give up possessions of; yield to another on compulsion; to give up or abandon, to give oneself up, as a prisoner, the act of surrendering

No sin can keep you separated from the grace of God. He loves sinners, has enough patience, and is waiting for the opportunity to transform your life. Your responsibility is to receive the grace of God.

You may wonder, "how God can save a person like me?" At times, you may have looked back on your life. You may have experienced heartaches, troubles, wasted time, wasted money and treated people inappropriately. This sermon by Dr. Stanley may transform your life. You don't need to give up. Dr. Stanley uses

St. Paul as an example of a bad person that He loved. God never gave up on him.

> *I give thanks to Christ Jesus our Lord, who has strengthened me, because He considered me faithful, appointing me to the ministry — one who was formerly a blasphemer, a persecutor, and an arrogant man. Since it was out of ignorance that I had acted in unbelief, I received mercy, and the grace of our Lord overflowed, along with the faith and love that are in Christ Jesus. This saying is trustworthy and deserving of full acceptance: "Christ Jesus came into the world to save sinners"-and I am the worst of them. But I received mercy because of this, so that in me, the worst [of them], Christ Jesus might demonstrate the utmost patience as an example to those who would believe in Him for eternal life. Now to the King eternal, immortal, invisible, the only God, be honor and glory forever and ever. Amen.*
> — 1 Timothy 1:12-17

> *And you were dead in your trespasses and sins 2 in which you previously walked according to this worldly age, according to the ruler of the atmospheric domain, the spirit now working in the disobedient. 3 We too all previously lived among them in our fleshly desires, carrying out the inclinations of our flesh and thoughts, and by nature we were children under wrath, as the others were also. 4 But God, who is abundant in mercy, because of His great love that He had for us, 5 made us alive with the Messiah even though we were dead in trespasses. By grace you are saved! 6 He also raised us up with Him and seated us with Him in the heavens, in Christ Jesus, 7 so that in the coming ages He might display the immeasurable riches of His grace in [His]*

kindness to us in Christ Jesus. 8 For by grace you are saved through faith, and this is not from yourselves; it is God's gift- 9 not from works, so that no one can boast. 10 For we are His creation-created in Christ Jesus for good works, which God prepared ahead of time so that we should walk in them.

— Ephesians 2:1-10

Another illustration of grace that Dr. Stanley recommends is Acts 9, which tells the story of Saul.

In closing, there is no sin that God cannot handle. Continuously, God is reaching out to His children, drawing them closer and closer. In times, God will reach down to shake things up, just to draw your attention. Yes, when bad things happen, it's God reaching out and shaking things up. That is how much He loves us. God's love is like a song, so extravagant, so unthinkable.

Dr. Stanley tells us not to claim to be religious by the blindness of God's love, trust, faithfulness, and kindness to human beings. God is waiting for you to make the most important decision of your life. One word — surrender.

God loves you, and this is His wish for you.

Dr. Charles Stanley – Sermon Notes – July 14, 2019 – GRACE ON DISPLAY – Part 2

Definition of Apostle – any of the disciples of Jesus, the original twelve, the leader of a new movement as in apostle Paul

There is only one way to receive the grace of God, and that is by accepting the Lord Jesus Christ as your savior. When you do that, something happens inside of you. Your attitude, your perspective on life, your lifestyle, the way you treat people, your humbleness, your gratitude, your thankfulness — they all change. God makes no mistakes, and everyone has the same opportunity when you become a believer in our Lord Jesus Christ. A new creation takes place, a new person with a new transformation for eternal life with our Heavenly Father. Grace changes everything. The apostle Paul was the work of God's grace. If God changed Paul, He could change you too.

Dr. Stanley shares the story of the apostle Paul and holds him up as an example of a sinner who turned his life over to our Lord Jesus Christ. Paul was a destroyer of people, even a murderer, before accepting Jesus as his savior. God reached down to Paul and said, "I will make you the most vocal disciple of Jesus Christ, now that you have accepted him as your Lord Jesus Christ." God can reach down to everyone, even murderers. This is the amazing power of our Heavenly Father.

When I came to you, brothers, announcing the testimony of God to you, I did not come with brilliance of speech or wisdom. For I determined to know nothing among you except Jesus Christ and Him crucified. And I was with you in weakness, in fear, and in much trembling. My speech and my proclamation were not with persuasive words of wisdom, but with a demonstration of the Spirit and power, so that your faith might not be based on men's wisdom but on God's power.

— 1 Corinthians 2:1-5

When was the last time you thanked God? When was the last time you served someone or something? Do not get so wrapped up in worldly stuff that you forget what God has done for you. Dr. Stanley says.

The only message that changes a person's life is the grace of God. Trust, obey, believe, live, work, and serve, so others will desire your newly transformed life. Grace changes the way you think and the way you live. It's not about me, myself, or I. Learn to help, love, and listen to others.

Dr. Stanley says you need to forget about yourself, and motivate and serve someone else, because the grace of God is living within you. You will understand, and you cannot keep it to yourself. You must share your blessings with others. You have been blessed so you may help others be blessed. Grace is greater than all sin. Remember, you are a chosen child of God, who reached down and became your savior. God does not seek payback when we sin.

Our job is to accept and trust our Lord Jesus Christ. Be attentive to attitude, humility, and action. God hates pride, Dr. Stanley teaches us, but rejoices in our humility. With action, there is a fair amount of suffering that we must endure. Our willingness to suffer is pleasing to God.

God loves you, and this is His wish for you.

Dr. Charles Stanley – Sermon Notes – July 21, 2019 – GRACE CHANGES EVERYTHING

By accepting Jesus Christ as your Savior, you immediately start to experience the amazing grace of God. You have a new life now. God has transformed us into the person He wants us to be. A new creation begins immediately. God makes no mistakes, and everyone has the same opportunity to experience this beautiful gift. You have now received from God the gifts of kindness, forgiveness, believing, gratitude, thankfulness, love, and service. Your old ways of thinking don't exist anymore. The grace of God cannot be hidden. Why? God has created a new person. Sometimes, God will put a block in your life because He loves you and has a gift for you — His grace. A new soul exists, and a new spirit exist. His beautiful gift sent from above — the grace of God.

> *Therefore, if anyone is in Christ, there is a new creation; old things have passed away, and look, new things have come. Now everything is from God, who reconciled us to Himself through Christ and gave us the ministry of reconciliation.*
> – 2 Corinthians 5:17-18

In Christ, we are a new creation! Grace is not about adding something to your life. Something must happen inside. When you accept the Lord Jesus Christ as your savior something magical takes place; you become a new person. By the grace of God, we can demonstrate our desire to serve Him, as well as our desire to show our new attitude, changed personality, and changed lifestyle. All of this is pleasing to God.

Research grace and its importance. By the grace of God, it's all the things you perhaps have been missing in life. God is waiting for your decision with open arms. Grace changes the way you think and live, and your love and kindness towards others. Be thankful and show humbleness that you have a second chance, the grace of God is a gift indeed. Stop and look at your life right now! Is this where you want to be? Don't miss out on the greatest gift of all, which is to spend eternity with our Lord Jesus Christ in Heaven.

God loves you, and this is His wish for you.

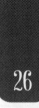

26

Dr. Charles Stanley - Sermon Notes – July 28, 2019 – THE RICHNESS OF GOD'S GRACE

Definition of Richness – owning much money or property; wealthy; well-supplied

Definition of Sanctified – holiness; holy; sacredness

Definition of Sacredness – sacred; consecrated to God; having to do with religion

Definition of Citizenship – a member of a state or nation who owes allegiance to it by birth or naturalization and is entitled to full civil rights

We are all heirs to the richness of God's grace the moment you become a child of God. This is by far the greatest gift of all. The richness of money cannot compare to the richness of God's grace. From birth, you are already in God's will. Therefore, as Christians, we must focus on grace and not on worldly money. When we die, we cannot take worldly money with us, but as a believer, we may be blessed with the richness of God's grace and blessed with eternity.

Please read the following passages, which provide clarification of this sermon:

> ...and if children, also heirs-heirs of God and co-heirs with Christ-seeing that we suffer with Him so that we may also be glorified with Him.
>
> – Romans 8:17

...but our citizenship is in heaven, from which we also eagerly wait for a Savior, the Lord Jesus Christ. He will transform the body of our humble condition into the likeness of His glorious body, by the power that enables Him to subject everything to Himself.

— Philippians 3:20-21

Do you not know that the unjust will not inherit God's kingdom? Do not be deceived: no sexually immoral people, idolaters, adulterers, male prostitutes, homosexuals, 10 thieves, greedy people, drunkards, revilers, or swindlers will inherit God's kingdom. 11 Some of you were like this; but you were washed, you were sanctified, you were justified in the name of the Lord Jesus Christ and by the Spirit of our God.

— 1 Corinthians 6:9-11

Start today, and ask yourself, "What is my relationship like with God?" Have you surrendered your life over to God? Do you trust that our Lord Jesus Christ died on the cross at Calvary and paid the price for all our sins?

It's important to note if you have made a request to God, and He has not responded to that request, it's because of His love for you. Everything that we possess comes from God and His plan for our life. God is in complete control, and He knows if danger is involved. Therefore, God has His reasons for not fulfilling your request. Allow God to pour out His love for you.

God loves you, and this is His wish for you.

27

Dr. Charles Stanley – Sermon Notes – August 4, 2019 – GOD'S SUSTAINING GRACE

Definition of Sustain – to keep in existence, maintain or prolong; to provide sustenance for; to carry the weight of; support; to endure, withstand; to comfort or encourage; to suffer; to uphold the validity; to confirm, corroborate

Definition of Enable – to make able; provide with means, power; to support the dysfunctional behavior of, as by compensating for it

Definition of Revelation – a revealing; a striking disclosure; disclosure to the humanity of divine truth

As a follower, how do you face your problems and respond to life? By the grace of God and understanding the importance of His sustaining grace. Grace is unearned and undeserved. As a child of God, when we accept our Lord Jesus Christ into our life, God will openly pour out His sustaining grace. Forgiveness, love, kindness, and helping others will appear in your life like never before.

Have you ever felt like you're living under an umbrella of out-of-control issues in your life? Dr. Stanley tells us there are times when everyone feels like this. Through His grace, God enables you to think and act differently towards these problems. He enables strength to drown out your weaknesses. As follower of our Lord Jesus Christ, it is your responsibility to believe in God's sustaining grace. God enables you to face conflict, pain, and suffering, but only if you are a follower. Otherwise, it is impossible to live by God's sustaining grace.

For if I want to boast, I will not be a fool, because I will be telling the truth. But I will spare you, so that no one can credit me with something beyond what he sees in me or hears from me, especially because of the extraordinary revelations. Therefore, so that I would not exalt myself, a thorn in the flesh was given to me, a messenger of Satan to torment me so I would not exalt myself. Concerning this, I pleaded with the Lord three times to take it away from me. But He said to me, "My grace is sufficient for you, for power is perfected in weakness."

— 2 Corinthians 12:6-9

By trusting God's sustaining grace, our weakness turns into strength, and this enables contentment in our lives. To live in contentment enables confidence, boldness, and self-control.

Keep asking, and it will be given to you. Keep searching, and you will find. Keep knocking, and the door will be opened to you. For everyone who asks receives, and the one who searches finds, and to the one who knocks, the door will be opened.

— Matthew 7:7-8

God doesn't always answer your prayer in the way you may want. God may give you a revelation that others do not receive. God may respond yes, no, or wait. The apostle Paul added another, "the power of God's grace is sufficient for me." What a beautiful, awesome gift it is to receive God's sustaining grace.

God may say to you, "The power of my Grace is sufficient for you."

God loves you, and this is His wish for you.

Dr. Charles Stanley – Sermon Notes – August 25, 2019 – THE KEY TO THE HEART OF GOD

Definition of Exact – characterized by or requiring accuracy, methodical; correct, precise; to demand, require

Definition of Partial – not complete, biased

Definition of Complete – full, whole, entire, thorough absolute, perfect; successfully execute

Obedience to God must be your priority to walk with God and be the person God desires you to be. Don't reject the voice of God, for God requires exact obedience and not a partial effort. There is no partial obedience, such as in "the Devil made me do it." Dr. Stanley teaches us that understanding God's obedience is the only way you will become happy.

The First Book of Samuel offers the best illustration of God, His power, and obedience vs. disobedience:

> *The Spirit of the Lord will control you, you will prophesy with them, and you will be transformed into a different person.*
> — 1 Samuel 10:6

The Spirit of the Lord will come powerfully on you. Read completely about the relationship between Saul and Samuel. Here you will feel the emotional power of God, and how He operates when you disobey. Some parts will be troublesome, but very true. Keep in mind that God is wise, and He makes no mistakes in His commands, especially when it comes to obedience and disobedience.

Obedience may be very painful in some circumstances. You may even convince yourself God is not interested in what you have to say or do. This is not true and is the Devil talking, not God. Our God is gracious, caring, and loving, and He is always interested in what you have to say and do. God is very active in our lives every day. Your job is to reach out, along with the guidance of the Holy Spirit, to receive His blessings and opportunities of obedience. Dr. Stanley would say, "Don't miss out on given opportunities." Allow the Holy Spirit to enable God's obedience, create a spirit of obedience, and honor it daily. Make it your number one priority to honor our Heavenly Father's spirit of obedience.

God is aware you may fail and miss His instructions. During these times, you should immediately stop, repent, and ask for God's forgiveness. He has promised to pick us up be there in times of need and restore our thinking on exact obedience and partial obedience.

Honor God with your obedience and follow the Lord wholeheartedly. God loves you, and you hold the key to God's heart when you honor His obedience.

God loves you, and this is His wish for you.

Dr. Charles Stanley – Sermon Notes – September 1, 2019 – THE KEY TO THE HEART OF GOD – STRENGTH OF OBEDIENCE

God has no bad plans for our lives, He only plans for the very best. God clearly outlines in the Bible how we are to show obedience to Him. Most people DO want to show their obedience to God, Dr. Stanley says. Jesus prayed daily in the early morning hours, he continues, and would slip away from the crowds to spend time in prayer. Jesus spent hours in fellowship with God and asking for strength in obedience.

> *But the news about Him spread even more, and large crowds would come together to hear Him and to be healed of their sicknesses. Yet He often withdrew to deserted places and prayed.*
> — Luke 5:15-16

Do you have a spirit of obedience? Is your fellowship right with God? Do you live your life by the "principles of obedience" or "preference of obedience?" Dr. Stanley encourages us to prioritize obedience by fellowship, Holy Spirit, and the will to believe. Find time during your day to fellowship with God. Learn to listen and lean on the word of the Holy Spirit that dwells inside. Pray for the will to believe in God's word. Fellowship, Holy Spirit, and belief are the perfect three principles of obedience. The Lord gave everyone availability to the Holy Spirit to help us along, and our job is to rely on the Holy Spirit to strengthen our obedience to our Heavenly Father.

Preference of obedience is what you want and not the desire of God. It is important to note there are temptations daily in our lives, some of which may be highly appealing. Pray to God when this happens and tell God you do not have the strength of obedience — be honest. Immediately rely on the Holy Spirit. God knows we do not live a perfect life, and that's why He sent the Holy Spirit.

It is helpful to read Philippians, Christ's Humility and Exaltation, which discusses the spirit of obedience and how you should obey to the point of death. It is a chronicle of what Jesus did when He came to earth.

Make your own attitude that of Christ Jesus,...
— Philippians 2:5

With the principles of obedience, there will be tears and sorrow to the point of asking God, "Why?" Expect sleepless night, filled with tears, crying out to God. The key is to develop strength is by understanding and following the principles of obedience — fellowship, Holy Spirit, and belief. When you obey, watch, and see what happens in your life. God only plans for the very best.

God loves you, and this is His wish for you.

30

Dr. Charles Stanley – Sermon Notes – September 8, 2019 – FIND THE STRENGTH TO OBEY GOD

God created us to fellowship with Him and live a life of obedience. It is impossible to walk with God, if we live a life of disobedience to Jesus Christ, Dr. Stanley teaches.

Jesus daily prayed in the early morning hours. He would slip away from crowds to spend time in prayer. Please don't miss your prayer time with God.

God is aware that you are weak, and temptation is appealing. It's during these times you must learn to rely on the Holy Spirit for guidance. Wait for your instruction from the Holy Spirit, our helper in life. Dr. Stanley tells us this will be painful, sorrowful, and tearful, along with sleepless nights. However, there is HOPE! Several scriptures in the Bible illustrate the pattern of Jesus' life, which is the key to your obedience. We are encouraged to study this. Are you willing to lay down your glory to walk with God? Jesus Christ did and humbled Himself to the point of death to be in obedience with the Father.

Do you have a spirit of obedience? Do you live by obedience or preference?

> *When evening came, after the sun had set, they began bringing to Him all those who were sick and those who were demon-possessed. The whole town was assembled at the door, and He healed many who were sick with various diseases and drove out many demons. But He*

would not permit the demons to speak, because they knew Him.

— Mark 1:32-34

But the news about Him spread even more, and large crowds would come together to hear Him and to be healed of their sicknesses. 16 Yet He often withdrew to deserted places and prayed.

— Luke 5:15-16

They, however, were filled with rage and started discussing with one another what they might do to Jesus.

— Luke 6:11

Jesus knew He had to follow these three principles, which you could say were His pattern of obedience — time to fellowship with the Father, reliance on the Holy Spirit, and a willingness to believe, obey and trust in God.

Nothing is more pleasing to God than when you obey and learn to develop a pattern of obedience to Him. We don't have to fall in disobedience to God. What matters to God is when you create your pattern of obedience. When this happens, you will be willing to lay down your glory to walk with God.

God loves you, and this is His wish for you.

31

Dr. Charles Stanley – Sermon Notes – September 15, 2019 – IF YOU LOVE ME, YOU WILL KEEP MY COMMANDMENTS

Definition of Command – to give an order, to have authority, an order; direction

Definition of Commandments – the act or power of commanding; something that is commanded

Definition of Obedience – obeying or willing to obey

The Ten Commandments

1. Do not have other gods besides Me.
2. Do not make an idol for yourself.
3. Do not misuse the name of the Lord your God.
4. Remember to dedicate the Sabbath day.
5. Honor your father and your mother.
6. Do not murder.
7. Do not commit adultery.
8. Do not steal.
9. Do not give false testimony against your neighbor.
10. Do not covet.

How much do you love God? How much are you willing to change your attitude and lifestyle to follow his commandments? Living a lifestyle that does not match God's obedience and commandments is hurtful to God and His heart. With God, there is no pick and choose. You cannot say you love God if you do not live a lifestyle of obedience following His Ten Commandments.

The love you have for God means that you choose a lifestyle of obedience, commandments, and the word.

Jesus loved you so much He died on the cross at Calvary and paid your sins in full so that you may have eternal life with your Heavenly Father. That's the greatest example of love.

> *If you love Me, you will keep My commandments. And I will ask the Father, and He will give you another Counselor to be with you forever. He is the Spirit of truth. The world is unable to receive Him because it doesn't see Him or know Him. But you do know Him, because He remains with you and will be in you.*
>
> — John 14:15-17

> *The one who has My commands and keeps them is the one who loves Me. And the one who loves Me will be loved by My Father. I also will love him and will reveal Myself to him.*
>
> — John 14:21

Be aware of your thoughts, your actions, and your strength at all times, Dr. Stanley teaches. You are to treat people the same way you want to be treated. Love is never halfway, but in full. An example of this, is when two people marry and say the words, "I do." Before this, Dr. Stanley says, there must be some facts laid out. What is your relationship and love for God like? Start your love and marriage out with a strong foundation and commitment to God, as well as yourself. Understand the Word of God, and what God expects of you, love and obedience. Build your marriage on a solid foundation, one of which is the wisdom to love correctly and live in obedience to God's word and commands. Make it a marriage that is rock solid and honors God in obedience and love. When we disobey, we are hurting the heart of God.

God loves you, and this is His wish for you.

32

Dr. Charles Stanley – Sermon Notes – September 22, 2019 – OBEDIENCE TO GOD

From the beginning to the end, God knows everything about you. Dr. Stanley says a wise person will honor a command from God no matter how small it may be. Disobeying a command from God will haunt you for the rest of your life. Every act and command are significant in the eyes of God. You may not see it, but when you obey a command from God, you receive God's blessing in return, as well as a blessing for others. A certain transformation takes place, enrichment happens. If you listen, you will hear God speak, "Obey me, and see what happens in your life." Allow God to enrich your life and show His blessing.

If you have been wronged by someone or something, Dr. Stanley teaches, you must forgive. It is always better to forgive first. When you forgive first, you are releasing your pain and suffering, as well as that of the wrongdoer. There is no room in your heart for hurtful memories. You are encouraged to live in the present and forget the past. As a believer, you do not need to look for approval from others. God wants you to lean and rely upon Him.

God loves you, and this is His wish for you.

33

Dr. Charles Stanley – Sermon Notes – October 6, 2019 – KNOW WHAT YOU BELIEVE

Always be ready to defend what you believe in. Don't let false teachers distract you. It matters greatly how you believe.

> *And who will harm you if you are passionate for what is good? But even if you should suffer for righteousness, you are blessed. Do not fear what they fear or be disturbed but set apart the Messiah as Lord in your hearts, and always be ready to give a defense to anyone who asks you for a reason for the hope that is in you.*
> *— 1 Peter 3:13-15*

Our Lord should be the Lord of your life. Believers must be ready to make a defense to those around them who may have doubts. People have the right to ask questions regarding their beliefs. Always respond and present yourself with gentleness. Use the best of your human reasoning. Be kind and choose your words wisely when you defend yourself. It makes all the difference in the world. This could be the perfect time to witness to someone. Dr. Stanley warns to be aware of false teachers.

> *But there were also false prophets among the people, just as there will be false teachers among you. They will secretly bring in destructive heresies, even denying the Master who bought them, and will bring swift destruction on themselves. Many will follow their unrestrained ways, and because of them the way of truth will be blasphemed. In their greed they will exploit you with deceptive words.*

Their condemnation, long ago, is not idle, and their destruction does not sleep.

— 2 Peter 2:1-3

You, therefore, my child, be strong in the grace that is in Christ Jesus. And what you have heard from me in the presence of many witnesses, commit to faithful men who will be able to teach others also.

— 2 Timothy 2:1-2

Develop a belief system that complies with the Word of God, which your life is directed by, and be prepared to make a defense how you believe.

Do not become a pick and choose type of person, Dr. Stanley says. Instead, establish a loyal belief in Christianity with Our Heavenly Father. There is no other God. Don't second guess what you were taught in the past. Focus on the future by developing your belief system and standing by it. Always be ready to defend yourself with gentleness. Learn to protect your mentality by developing a strong belief system of Bible truth. The grid of your thinking needs to line up with your lifestyle, faith, and belief system; they must be in sequence with each other.

Mothers and fathers, instruct your children to be strong and establish what you believe in early. Always search for the Bible's truth.

God loves you, and this is His will for you.

34

Dr. Charles Stanley – Sermon Notes – October 20, 2019 – OUR BURNING BUSHES

When God speaks to you, how do you respond? Dr. Stanley explains what Moses did in his time of "burning bushes," which is covered in Exodus 3:1-6.

We all have experienced "burning bushes," Dr. Stanley says. Certain experiences in our life may come unexpectedly. These experiences will present challenges or may offer powerful greatness. What you accomplish in life can only be accomplished on your knees in prayer. God speaks to everyone differently. Not everyone receives the same challenges from God. Our responsibility is to listen when God speaks. You may or may not like what God has to say, however, these experiences may turn into moments to last a lifetime.

> *No weapon formed against you will succeed, and you will refute any accusation raised against you in court. This is the heritage of the Lord's servants, and their righteousness is from Me. This is the Lord's declaration.*
> *– Isaiah 54:17*

God knows everything and everybody. God allows only what is the best for you. Step by step, He will walk with you in all your decisions, but only if you listen, only if you trust, and only if you believe in Him.

What you accomplish in life can only be accomplished on your knees. When you go to pray on your knees, you are recognizing God. You honor, trust, and understand His power and authority.

Be thankful to God and praise Him in the highest.

God loves you, and this is His wish for you.

35

Dr. Charles Stanley – Sermon Notes – October 27, 2019 – KNOW WHAT YOU BELIEVE – Part 2

The Church, and living a Christian Life, is the most precious journey that God has given you! You may ask yourself, "Why do I need to go to church?" The church is where you can study the word of God and learn the importance of the body of Christ. It's meeting with a group of people who trust Jesus Christ as their savior. When this happens, you learn to develop your belief system. You study who is the Father, who is Jesus Christ, and who is the Holy Spirit, all three in one.

Do church people have their share of problems? Of course, they do. The comfort of talking and interacting with others is gratifying and offers encouragement to one another. God already knows you have hardship and troubles, but it's through His word and attending church that you can obtain wisdom, peace, and comfort. The Holy Spirit dwells in you and has sealed you as a child of God. Dr. Stanley says the Bible is both hard and easy to read. He encourages new believers to start reading in the Book of John. Soak your mind in the Bible; it cleanses your soul and refreshes your spirit. Share what God has done in your life with others, share your faith with others, give yourself to others, and be willing to serve. The Holy Spirit will give you the confidence to hold onto the word of God just when you seek advice. Please, don't neglect the Bible. Find time for reading and studying the Bible.

Who are you as a child of God? You have two orders that we must obey for salvation, Dr. Stanley teaches. The first is that you must be Baptized. When you are saved your old life is buried, and you obtain a new spirit and a new life. Your character changes, you are reborn, and you immediately are a child of the living God. "I in you, you in me" the Bible tells us. Baptism is an expression of obedience. Baptism is a time for great celebration. Once you receive Jesus Christ as your savior, you grow up. He matures you, grows your grace, and grows your intimacy. You become a disciple, share, serve others, trust and believe, obey, and walk in the light of Jesus Christ through His love and grace. You become like Jesus Christ, offering our love and kindness as you serve and help others in need. Most importantly, you become a better person. The second order that you must obey is to pray, devote yourself to reading the Bible, and find your time and your place of worship. Don't miss out on the journey of Christianity.

Allow God to polish and shine you up!

The Christian life is Jesus Christ living His life in us.

God loves you, and this is His wish for you.

36

Dr. Charles Stanley – Sermon Notes – November 3, 2019 – KNOW WHAT YOU BELIEVE – Part 3

Your belief system affects everything you do in your life. Dr. Stanley says it can sometimes feel as if Satan is winning as a destroyer in our lives. Do not be fooled by the ways of Satan. Always be willing and able to make a defense about your belief system. Some may not know this, but Satan was created as a person, as well as an angel, and he desired to be equal with God. Therefore, Satan was always rebelling against God. Two words come to mind — right vs. wrong. What is the right belief system? What is the wrong belief system? Satan operates with the wrong belief system. Satan's foundation is division, deceit, and destruction. Minute by minute, Satan operates with the mindset of attacking and destroying believers and doing as much damage as possible. Satan is out to ruin as many lives as he possibly can. You must stand firm in your belief system. Don't allow Satan to counterfeit our Kingdom. Know that Satan will do whatever he can to win you over, but don't be fooled by his actions. Always rely on the Word of God. He loves you and has the best plan for you.

> *Therefore, get your minds ready for action, being self-disciplined, and set your hope completely on the grace to be brought to you at the revelation of Jesus Christ. As obedient children, do not be conformed to the desires of your former ignorance but, as the One who called you is holy, you also are to be holy in all your conduct; for it is written, Be holy, because I am holy.*
> — 1 Peter 1:13-16.

"Desires of your former ignorance," what does this mean? It means lying or instant gratification. It's a feel-good emotion to have it now and indulge in your desires.

> *Blessed is the one who reads and blessed are those who hear the words of this prophecy and keep what is written in it, because the time is near! John: To the seven churches in the province of Asia. Grace and peace to you from the One who is, who was, and who is coming; from the seven spirits before His throne; and from Jesus Christ, the faithful witness, the firstborn from the dead and the ruler of the kings of the earth. To Him who loves us and has set us free from our sins by His blood, and made us a kingdom, priests to His God and Father-to Him be the glory and dominion forever and ever. Amen. Look! He is coming with the clouds, and every eye will see Him, including those who pierced Him. And all the families of the earth will mourn over Him. This is certain. Amen. "I am the Alpha and the Omega," says the Lord God, "the One who is, who was, and who is coming, the Almighty."*
>
> – Revelation 1:3-8

Welcome God into your life, surrender to him, be ridden of sin, and experience the greatest gift to mankind — the gift of eternal life with our Heavenly Father, our Lord Jesus Christ.

Make the decision today about what is going to be your eternal destiny. Because the time is near!

God loves you, and this is His wish for you.

Dr. Charles Stanley – Sermon Notes – November 10, 2019 – LIFE'S TRIALS AND EXPERIENCES

You must learn and understand why God allows things to happen in your life. Situations that you do not understand. When circumstances arise in your life that are painful, sorrowful, unbelievable, or disappointing, it's because God is testing your Faith. God wants to strengthen you, if you will, to build you up, so you can deal with those situations when they appear. What is God up to? He is building your character and testing your faith, all at the same time, in difficult storms.

Dr. Stanley shares an example of God testing his faith when he receives a telephone call — the worst of his life — with unbelievable news. He did not respond with rage, fear, or denial. He immediately put his trust in God and said, "God is in control of everything." This may sound simple, but this is exactly how God works. There is nothing simple about God. He is testing your faith in bad situations to build you up. God knows how to get your attention. In some instances, your vision becomes blurred, and things become messed up, thus leading you to the one person who can help — God. His will is for you to always rely on and trust in Him.

> *Blessed be the God and Father of our Lord Jesus Christ. According to His great mercy, He has given us a new birth into a living hope through the resurrection of Jesus Christ from the dead, and into an inheritance that is imperishable, uncorrupted, and unfading, kept in heaven for you, who are being protected by God's power through*

faith for a salvation that is ready to be revealed in the last time. You rejoice in this, though now for a short time you have had to be distressed by various trials so that the genuineness of your faith-more valuable than gold, which perishes though refined by fire-may result in praise, glory, and honor at the revelation of Jesus Christ. You love Him, though you have not seen Him. And though not seeing Him now, you believe in Him and rejoice with inexpressible and glorious joy, because you are receiving the goal of your faith, the salvation of your souls.

— 1 Peter 1:3-9

Sometimes the purpose of these trials is beyond you. God is going to deal with your sins one way or another. He will test to see if your faith is a reliable one. That's how much He loves you. God allows everyone to have ups and downs. Did you know it's okay to tell God you are afraid and need His help? He is building your character and testing your faith, all at the same time, to be fit for His Kingdom.

It's written in the Bible that your faith is more valuable than gold.

God loves you, and this is His wish for you.

Dr. Charles Stanley – Sermon Notes – November 17, 2019 – LIFE'S TRIALS EXPLAINED

Definition of Confirmation – to undergo religious confirmation; to bring into an agreement; to act following accepted rules, customs

Definition of Process – a continuing development involving many changes; a method of doing something with all steps involved

Definition of Tailor – one who makes repairs; to form for a certain purpose; a designer

Definition of Purpose – to intend or plan; something one intends to get or do; determination, by design, intentionally, purposeful

Godly men and women through tough times understand that hardship, pain, suffering, and tears are how God operates. He operates this way to build you up and to improve your character. After these trials, you will be able to take leaps toward God.

To confirm, God's goal is to conform you to the likeness of His son Jesus Christ. There is danger if you draw a line between God and His instructions to conform, Dr. Stanley warns. When you become a Christian, you give up all rights to Him and now you belong to Him. Your purpose in life is not about richness and fame, it's about God molding you into a Christian. He created you to be in the beginning as a character without sin.

It's pleasing to God when you demonstrate your character to be that of Jesus Christ, who is in all your activities. He is shaping and molding you daily. Before they became saved, many will admit they all had some rough edges.

In the process and purpose, God will use the proof of your faith. Do you trust that God is in control of everything? Do you trust that God will not give you more than you can handle? Just when you may say, "God, that is enough, no more" don't be surprised when God increases your hardship, pain, suffering, and tears. God will only give you what you can handle. When God increases your trials, He is telling you that you're not built up the way He wants you to be. When developing a Godly character, you can expect He will put limitations on your lifestyle. God's goal is for you to be tailored like a perfect suit.

God's will for you is not to resist difficult times but welcome them. You may say no. However, in the end, if you trust the process, purpose, and confirmation, you will be saying yes! Most importantly, thank God for pulling you through.

God loves you, and this is His wish for you.

Dr. Charles Stanley – Sermon Notes – November 24, 2019 – A THANKFUL HEART

Dr. Stanley asked what it means to have a grateful heart. Are you a thankful person or do you find yourself complaining? Your thanksgiving starts with the human heart. It is the seed that has been planted by our Heavenly Father. Daily, your seed grows based on the way you develop a personal relationship with God, develop a way to study the Bible, develop compassion for others, and develop choices in your life. It also grows based on how you serve and give to others, your attitude, and love and cherish your family and friendships.

> Shout triumphantly to the Lord, all the earth. Serve the Lord with gladness; come before Him with joyful songs. Acknowledge that the Lord is God. He made us, and we are His - His people, the sheep of His pasture. Enter His gates with thanksgiving and His courts with praise. Give thanks to Him and praise His name. For the Lord is good, and His love is eternal; His faithfulness endures through all generations.
> – Psalms 100

God showed thanksgiving, love, and gratitude when He sent His only son, Jesus Christ, to perish on the cross to pay in full your debt of sins and give you eternal life with our Heavenly Father. What is your real motivation for gratitude? Do you serve and believe in one God? Do you trust and believe He is a sovereign God? Do you trust and believe He is the ruler of our universe? Do you believe He is our one and only savior? God's love is unconditional. He is a forgiving God, and He is a promising God. God is with you morning, noon, and night, and has promised never to leave. God adopted you, and now you are His child. It is a seal. God has gifted you with certain skills that fit your personality. Your job is to cherish those skills and show gratitude! God plans to allow everyone the very best in life. One day, God is going to call your name, and it will be a day of joyfulness. Dr. Stanley says you will be limited on how you think about Heaven and what you will be doing. That too is God's plan for you — eternal life. You can turn to the Book of Revelation to learn more about Heaven.

Praise God and pray, "Thank you, God. Thank you, God." Protect your thankful heart and watch your seed grow.

God loves you, and this is His wish for you.

40

Dr. Charles Stanley – Sermon Notes – December 1, 2019 – A THANKFUL HEART – Part 2

Is your mind focused on the truthfulness of what it means to have a grateful heart? Or is your mind filled with negativity and complaining? Thankful people have a heart that is like a fountain, overflowing with gratitude and thanksgiving. A grateful heart is always shining and walking in the ways of our Lord Jesus Christ. You simply cannot deny a thankful heart. Thankful people are happier and healthier even when times are difficult. God allows certain things to happen in your life. You are to allow God to handle your battles for you. God wants you to focus on these spiritual battles and give thanks to them. He is watching and waiting to see your reaction. He wants to see if your motivation is correct. God created your awesome bodies and instilled His promises in you so you may become like His son Jesus Christ and be eternally grateful.

> *Don't worry about anything, but in everything, through prayer and petition with thanksgiving, let your requests be made known to God. And the peace of God, which surpasses every thought, will guard your hearts and your minds in Christ Jesus.*
>
> – Philippians 4:6-7

A grateful heart clears the way and motivates you to live a better life and a better lifestyle. It's a developing and cleansing process of who you are. A grateful heart leans towards God's real purpose for you in life. God knows you will go through heartaches and temptations; however, a thankful heart understands and will look for a purpose. A grateful heart will bring you to submission even when you don't fully understand. God's purpose is for you to show your dependence on Him to pull you through difficult and unpleasant situations you face. With God there is no pride and no arrogance. Everyone is equal in God's eyes. God does not waste time, and He knows exactly what to do and when to do it. God's purpose is to show you His love for His Son, our Lord Jesus Christ, and not about you. God constantly reminds you to always depend and lean on Him and in all situations. All people are sinners, but it's through Jesus Christ and by His grace that you can change your life. Sometimes it's difficult to be thankful, but you must press on and give thanks even if you don't feel like doing so. Be thankful and serve God with thanksgiving at all times. A thankful heart is always an attractive heart. Allow your thankful heart to shine for you!

God loves you, and this is His wish for you.

41

Dr. Charles Stanley – Sermon Notes – December 8, 2019 - LIFTING THE WEIGHT OF HEAVY BURDENS

Definition of Burden — anything that is carried; load, heavy load; as of work, care, or duty, capacity; oppress

There is no question you carry a certain amount of burden and sin in your life. When the heavy burden of guilt is ignored, Dr. Stanley says, it soon becomes a mental health issue. An emotional kind of sickness takes place in your body. Carrying this guilt is like carrying a heavy rock around. It's a heavy weight in your heart that is not healthy. Guilt will zap your energy and deplete your motivation abilities, as well as interfere with your thinking process. Sin operates in the same manner, but it is much worse. Sin affects a person's health, family, friends, home, finances, career, and much more.

When you become confused about our burden and sin, you must ask yourself, "What is the cause of these burdens and sins? Where are they coming from?" Dr. Stanley describes burden in three ways — prolific burden, burden by God, and daily burden. However, it is important to know that God does not want us to carry these burdens alone.

> *Come to Me, all of you who are weary and burdened, and I will give you rest. All of you, take up My yoke and learn from Me, because I am gentle and humble in heart, and you will find rest for yourselves. For My yoke is easy and My burden is light.*
> — Mathew 11:28-30

Cast your burden on the Lord, and He will support you;
He will never allow the righteous to be shaken. You,
God, will bring them down to the pit of destruction; men
of bloodshed and treachery will not live out half their
days. But I will trust in You.

– Psalms 55:22-23

There are days when you may say, "God, I cannot handle this burden." It's days like this when you must turn to your faith and trust in God. It's the only way to receive relief from your burdens and sins. Leave all your burdens at God's feet, especially when your emotions, burdens, and sins get the best of you. Look at what Jesus did for us on the Cross at Calvary. He perished and carried everyone's burdens and sins. He paid the price so you may spend eternal life with your Lord Jesus Christ. He carried all that weight for you and me. That's how much God loves us. Yes, cast your burden on the Lord, for He indeed will lift the weight of your heavy burdens. Your responsibility is to have faith and trust in Him.

God loves you, and this is His wish for you.

42

Dr. Charles Stanley – Sermon Notes –
December 22, 2019 – THE BIRTH OF JESUS

Definition of Significant – having or expressing a meaning; a special or hidden one; full of meaning; important

God has a plan and purpose for your life, and you are very significant to Him. God knows exactly where you are, and you are somebody. It's very important to understand that God does not only use believers, but unbelievers are just as important. Look at the story of the birth of Jesus. He was born in a then-insignificant place called Bethlehem (not Rome). He was born in a stable and placed in a cattle feeder, not a controlled environment. His father was a carpenter and his mother a homemaker, both seemingly regular people, and His birth came as a complicated miracle, but was otherwise insignificant. Little did we know the creator of the world was just born.

Jesus Christ, the Son of God, died on the cross and forgave all our sins, so we may have the opportunity to spend eternal life in heaven. This message is so important, and you can not keep it to yourself. Do you have the courage to spread this amazing news to your co-workers and neighbors? "What is holding you back?" Dr. Stanley asks. Jesus' birth is the wake-up call to the world to get ready for eternity. Please, don't miss this opportunity to spread this incredible news to others!

God will use ungodly, seemingly insignificant people to achieve His plan and purpose. God has been using ungodly people for years. Dr. Stanley mentions the legal system and the evilness we witness. We must not be fooled by these haters and evildoers. You must trust and obey what God has ordered. He is always in control.

God knows when you are experiencing darkness, loneliness, and rejection. He also knows these emotions are temporary. God loves you and has a better plan for you! God is building you up to walk in His ways and His grace. Love one another, trust, believe, joy, peace, sharing, kindness, forgiveness — this is how significant you are to God. He has promised to protect you.

Jesus Christ is the Lord of your life. The Bible states, "For God so loved…" You are to rewrap that love and give it to others, even the ungodly and seemingly insignificant.

God loves you, and this is His wish for you.

Dr. Charles Stanley – Sermon Notes – December 29, 2019 – OBEYING GOD IS A SERIOUS DECISION

Obeying God is not an option. It is an essential command from Him. Obedience is the trademark you give to yourself. It is who you are as a person, as well as the way you live. God is very serious when He commands obedience. God is your creator. He instructs you with every heartbeat until death to stay in obedience of His commands. God has the right to control and enforce all laws. Disobedience, on the other hand, is a profound problem. God's command will result in an evil curse. It will be the direct calling of God for punishment.

> *Obey the Lord your God and follow His commands and statutes I am giving you today.*
> *— Deuteronomy 27:10*

> *Now if you faithfully obey the Lord your God and are careful to follow all His commands, I am giving you today, the Lord your God will put you far above all the nations of the earth.*
> *— Deuteronomy 28:1*

> *All these curses will come, pursue, and overtake you until you are destroyed, since you did not obey the Lord your God and keep the commands and statutes, He gave you.*
> *— Deuteronomy 28:45*

Is your mindset that you can do it yourself and don't need anyone's help?

> So, Jesus said to them, "When you lift up the Son of Man, then you will know that I am [He], and that I do nothing on My own. But just as the Father taught Me, I say these things. The One who sent Me is with Me. He has not left Me alone, because I always do what pleases Him."
>
> — John 8:28-29

God sent the Holy Spirit to dwell within you. He is your guide to compliance with your Heavenly Father and His commandments. You are to trust, obey, and listen to the Holy Spirit when He speaks. You cannot live a Godly life without the Holy Spirit. The Holy Spirit enables in you the power to make the right decisions. You must listen and follow His commands.

Dr. Stanley says it is essential to always stay focused on Jesus Christ. When you fail to do so, the Devil will derail your thinking and your life will take a turn for the worst. When you disobey, you are breaking the heart of God.

God loves you, and this is His wish for you.

Dr. Charles Stanley – Sermon Notes – January 5, 2020 – HOLDING ONTO HOPE

Holding onto hope requires prayer and talking directly to the Lord. Why is prayer so important? God loves you, and He has the power to turn your hope into reality. Never give up hope! God says, "Bring all your hopes and dreams to Me, and never surrender nor lay them down".

One of the best stories in the Bible to gain a better understanding is 1 Samuel – Hannah's Story.

There is something about prayer, acknowledging the power of God, and realizing how He can alter your life instantly. Having great faith and hopes sometimes may take years, Dr. Stanley explains. However, you must stick with your hope and dreams, even if everyone else tells you to stop. Never give in to what others say. Do not listen and allow them to steal your hopes and dreams — maintain your perseverance. You must trust God under all circumstances and refuse to give up. In doing so, God has promised to answer them one by one.

God has a plan to answer your hopes and dreams and what you desire. Sometimes He has a bigger and better plan for you. God never gives you less than what you ask, and He will only give you the very best. He will increase your hopes and dreams, not decrease them. You don't have to be perfect in God's eyes, because He knows we all make mistakes. God knows your mistakes, doubts, and frustrations in life. Do not let the Devil drag you down to hopelessness.

All your answers and questions are found directly by reading the Bible. God promises He will bring you out of turmoil. The moment you accept Him as your savior, He will restore your hope, faith, and perseverance. God does not want you to be hopeless.

God loves you, and this is His wish for you.

Dr. Charles Stanley – Sermon Notes – January 12, 2020 – UNDERSTANDING THE CALL OF GOD

Be thankful today! Sooner or later God is going to be calling upon you and me. Don't miss your call from God. He speaks clearly and is not into the mystery business. It's very important to note there are consequences if you fail to listen to God. Therefore, when God calls you, we pay attention and listen up. There are times you may not understand when God is calling. For more on the relationship between God and yourself, read 1 Samuel – Samuel's Call.

When you hear God's voice and His command, you are to respond, "Speak, Lord for your servant is listening." Everyone gets a call from God, Dr. Stanley says, and it's normal to respond, "God, this does not fit into my plan. I'm confused and don't understand. I was not expecting this type of task." Did you know God is a perfectionist? God will not give you a task that you cannot handle. There are four ways you can respond to God's calling — yes, no, not now, or ignore it completely. Well, God has a way to get your attention, especially if you are running too fast. God may put a disastrous situation in your life, laying you down flat to the point of desperation, pain, and suffering. Use your wisdom when you hear a call from God, which is always personal. He loves you and will speak to you quietly. God is always watching, listening, and waiting for you to respond. God may use other people to assist you in developing the right relationship with Jesus Christ. Please, don't let God down.

Dr. Stanley has questions for parents — "Are you building a foundation and environment for your children in the home today? Are your children listening to God when He speaks to them? Mom and Dad, when was the last time you got down on your knees in prayer? Did your children see this?" Yes, down on your knees by your bed. Parents must develop a guidance system for their children. Otherwise, your children will miss out on what God is all about, His love for them, and how they are to conduct themselves. Children are not born with these instructions, so they must be taught by both parents. Children love to watch and act as their parents, so it's critical you set the foundation. Do this and watch your children experience the greatest gifts of all — God's love and salvation.

God loves you, and this is His wish for you.

**Dr. Charles Stanley – Sermon Notes – February
2, 2020 – WHEN IT'S WISE TO WAIT**

Do you often find yourself pushing and shoving ahead of God? Please, do not make a big mistake by relying on your timing and schedule instead of God's. Did you know, in some instances, God will allow us to do it our way, and He knows it's going to turn into a disappointment? Trusting and obeying are commands from God. You are to pause and wait for His further instructions. How do you do this? Be still, wait upon God to respond, and listen to His instruction.

> *Wait for the Lord; be courageous and let your heart be strong. Wait for the Lord.*
> — Psalms 27:14

Dr. Stanley warns to avoid being impatient. Keep calm, pause, and wait for God's instructions. Cherish moment by moment the anticipation of God's will.

The rewards of waiting are discovery of God's purpose is, learning to trust God, and receiving supernatural and physical strength. In addition, you will win the Battle of Life, receive the "big" answers to your prayers, fulfillment in our faith, and insight to God is working on your behalf. God tells you, "I will wait, and you will wait."

> *He gives strength to the weary and strengthens the powerless.*
> — Isaiah 40:29

When you become impatient, you also become worn out and weary. This is why you need God on your team. Your team is composed of trust, obedience, waiting, and prayer. Our Heavenly Father understands there will be temptations and the desire to have your way on your schedule. However, you must realize that is not God speaking; it is the Devil speaking to lure you in.

How do you know God is on your team? Christians who wait upon God and His instructions keep going and going. Christians yield to obedience and prayer, they do not become impatient, and they do not push before God. God is on your team He is on your side when you wait for His directions. There is absolutely no gain when you move ahead of God, only a huge amount of loss. When you do not see answers to your prayers, it's because you're focused on your schedule and not God's. His timing is always the right time because He has a specific reason. Please, do not frustrate God. Keep calm, demonstrate obedience and trust, and wait upon God, who is never early or late. He knows the exact time to intervene. God tells you, "Do not worry. Let me take care of the consequences of your obedience." God already knows what you endure when waiting upon Him. You will be tested by faith, humility, patience, courage, and certain fears. Therefore, you must wait for God's timing!

What happens when you do not wait for God? You are out of God's will and miss His opportunity. There is pain, not only for you but for others. You may suffer a financial loss, as well as confusion in your life. You must wait for God and His direction. Allow God to become your best mediator and fight the battle of life for you on His schedule.

God loves you, and this is His wish for you.

Dr. Charles Stanley – Sermon Notes –
February 9, 2020 – SPIRITUAL BLINDNESS

The ultimate spiritual blindness is when we walk in darkness, Dr. Stanley says. Don't put yourself in the very dangerous situation of picking and choosing against the Word of God. It's critical to understand that Satan's main objective is to attack the Word of God. Satan's evilness is to blind the minds of mankind by brainwashing men and women to doubt God's authority and God's power.

The signs of spiritual blindness are in your attitude. For example, insisting on doing things your way, as well as believing no one can tell you what you can and cannot do. Do you like to be a rebellious person? Does pride stand in your way? Is there another religion you believe in? This type of behavior and attitude starts small, but over time Satan will wear you down and weaken your spiritual mind. It's like having tape over your eyes and the sun cannot shine through. You are telling God you do not believe in His word and choose to walk in darkness.

Satan's objective is to attack and destroy every good thing that comes along. Please, do not move in Satan's direction. It is his biggest lie and results in the total spiritual blindness of a person. Satan is determined when it comes to spiritual blindness, especially when believers are attacked.

When a nation of unbelievers gathers, Dr. Stanley explains, they may push misinformation that the Bible has many errors, causing people to become saturated with doubt. Do not teach others that the Bible is full of errors.

Spiritual blindness leads to separation from your Heavenly Father. Our eternal destiny is to live in the Lake of the Fire in darkness.

> It is written: "'As surely as I live,' says the Lord, 'every knee will bow before me; every tongue will acknowledge God.'" So then, each of us will give an account of ourselves to God.
> — Romans 14:11-12

Do not bow down to Satan and move in his misdirection.

> But whenever anyone turns to the Lord, the veil is taken away. Now the Lord is the Spirit, and where the Spirit of the Lord is, there is freedom. And we all, who with unveiled faces contemplate the Lord's glory, are being transformed into his image with ever-increasing glory, which comes from the Lord, who is the Spirit.
> — 2 Corinthians 3:16-18

God keeps his promises when we surrender our lives over to Him. He is the only one that can and will prevent our spiritual blindness. Allow God to work in your life so you are walking in the sunshine and not darkness.

God loves you, and this is His wish for you.

Dr. Charles Stanley – Sermon Notes – February 16, 2020 – BREAKING THE PROCESS

Why do you keep running away from God when He is looking for you? Is it because you choose to do things your way and you are self-centered? Maybe you choose the stereotype of being macho. Can it be that it feels better to rebel instead of surrendering? Could it be you do not like nor love yourself enough? Is it because you do not feel worthy of His blessings? Why do you choose to protest what God has to offer, which is eternal life with Him in heaven? God is looking for you, but you just keep running away!

God has a tool He uses to draw people near called the "breaking process." God targets you and puts the pressure on because He loves you and wants only the very best. God may use other people or an incident that cause pain and suffering. Why in the world would you continue to rebel and reject God's salvation? Why would you continue to manipulate and use your escape tools? In the story of Jonah, Dr. Stanley explains, God demonstrates His unbelievable authority and power. He created the winds to be so strong in a sea storm that Jonah overboard and was swallowed by a whale. This all happened because Jonah was running from God. God had no other choice to bring pressure upon Jonah. Therefore, God used a storm and a whale as His breaking process to save Jonah.

> *Jonah prayed to the Lord his God from inside the fish: I called to the Lord in my distress, and He answered me. I cried out for help in the belly of Sheol; You heard my voice. You threw me into the depths, into the heart of*

the seas, and the current overcame me. All Your breakers and Your billows swept over me.

But I said: I have been banished from Your sight, yet I will look once more toward Your holy temple. The waters engulfed me up to the neck; the watery depths overcame me; seaweed was wrapped around my head. I sank to the foundations of the mountains; the earth with its prison bars closed behind me forever! But You raised my life from the Pit, Lord my God!

As my life was fading away, I remembered the Lord. My prayer came to You, to Your holy temple. Those who cling to worthless idols forsake faithful love, but as for me, I will sacrifice to You with a voice of thanksgiving. I will fulfill what I have vowed. Salvation is from the Lord! Then the Lord commanded the fish, and it vomited Jonah onto dry land.

—Jonah 2:1-10

It is foolish not to have God's hand in our life when He is behind us all the way.

There is a big price to pay when we resist God's will Dr. Stanley says, such as family separation, endangerment to someone else you love dearly the loss of financial status, estrangement from you and God, and other negative consequences. Don't allow this overwhelming amount of fear and pain in your life just because you want things done your way. A foolish person cannot gain and only loses when rebelling and refusing God's will.

Parents who do not set an example of God's great love and His desire for salvation force their children to bear the weight of the parent's sins and carry it with them for the rest of their lives.

Children do not deserve to carry this enormous burden of guilt and shame.

The clock is ticking and someday it will be too late. God may say, "Ok, you win and have run from me. It is time to put you on the shelf." Please, do not let this happen, and allow God to use His breaking process on you, just as He did in Jonah's case. You may experience the greatest gift of all — eternity with our Heavenly Father.

Perhaps today will be the day you stop running from God and surrender.

God loves you, and this is His wish for you.

Dr. Charles Stanley – Sermon Notes – February 23, 2020 - PURSUING GOD'S HEART – HOW GOD CHOOSES

Did you know God has specific questions for you to ask yourself? Will you be ready when God calls? What are you doing to prepare yourself? God does not look to the perfect family nor a family of wealth. God is looking at the character of a person's heart. In his lifetime, Dr. Stanley has seen brilliant men and women come and go, who unfortunately fizzled out. Their foundation was not ready or strong enough because they failed to be ready for God's call.

Dr. Stanley talks about King David, who was least favored to be the King of Israel. He had a reddish complexion, light hair, and was the least popular of his siblings. David was from a great tribe and the son of Jesse. David was colorful and a poet. He would sleep under the stars and face the elements. However, David was an outlaw, a sinner, an adulterer, and a murderer. God knew David would fall and that he struggled with rejection. David was running from his life, but he could not run from God. Through all the hardships, God was preparing and prepping David to be the King of Israel. When the Holy Spirit came upon David, he was immediately equipped and ready to serve God.

> *My heart, O God, is steadfast, my heart is steadfast; I will sing and make music.*
> — Psalms 57:7

How does God choose people? He looks at the character of a person's heart and chooses people contrary to human reason. God is not interested in your appearance. He wants to know what you have been doing to get ready, for His calling. Interestingly to note, here is the difference between man and God. A man looks towards appearance, God looks at the character of your heart. He knows your foolishness, but sees your potential, which is far greater than any foolishness. God is in the business of looking at your character not your outer beauty.

Parents encourage their children to excel, study harder, and give their very best all the way through college, Dr. Stanley says, but their kids may wipe out. God looks at their character, potential, and will for God to equip them. To the students, I remind you to hold up to your responsibility and remember God is prepping you for a future you can be proud of and a career you can say you worked hard for. However, those dreams will fade if your character and heart are not right with God. It's your responsibility to make those dreams come true.

God is preparing everyone for something. Is He preparing you for a promotion? Is God preparing you for a child? Could it be a godly man is looking for a godly woman or vice versa? Whatever it is, you must be ready. Heartbreaking to say, but if you are not read, God may say, I chose someone else because they were. God loves you so very much and wants to say, "I chose you because you were ready."

God loves you, and this is His wish for you.

50

Dr. Charley Stanley – Sermon Notes – March 1, 2020 – PURSING GOD'S HEART – MOTIVATION TO CHALLENGE GIANTS

We all at one time or another have had giants in our life we must face, as well as circumstances with others that can be downright fearful. What giant is in your life? Dr. Stanley asks. Do you know what it is? Have you identified what it is?

The first thing you must do is to identify the problem. What exactly is the barrier that keeps you running away from God? Is God or is Satan in control? Be specific and analyze the situation. As a Christian, you are to honor and obey God and realize that He is always in charge. There is no reason to be fearful or to run away from God. When you fail at something in your life, it is Satan challenging God's plan for your life. It is your responsibility to read the Bible and lean on God when these giants appear. Immediately tell Satan, "I chose to lean on God."

To understand this better, Dr. Stanley recommends to read 1 Samuel 17 — David vs. Goliath.

> *"Your servant has killed lions and bears; this uncircumcised Philistine will be like one of them, for he has defied the armies of the living God." Then David said, "The Lord who rescued me from the paw of the lion and the paw of the bear will rescue me from the hand of this Philistine."*
> – 1 Samuel 17:36–37

David identified the problem — God vs. no God in Israel. Even though he was a youth, David was intelligent, healthy, and handsome.

Goliath said to David, "Am I a dog that you come against me with sticks? Then he cursed David by his gods. "Come here," the Philistine called to David, "and I'll give your flesh to the birds of the sky and the wild beasts!" David said to the Philistine: "You come against me with a sword, spear, and javelin, but I come against you in the name of the Lord of Armies, the God of the ranks of Israel – you have defied him. Today, the Lord will hand you over to me. Today, I'll strike you down, remove your head, and give the corpses of the Philistine camp to the birds of the sky and the wild creatures of the earth. Then all the world will know that Israel has a God, and this whole assembly will know that it is not by sword or by spear that the Lord saves, for the battle is the Lord's. He will hand you over to us." When the Philistine started forward to attack him, David ran quickly to the battle line to meet the Philistine. David put his hand in the bag, took out a stone, slung it, and hit the Philistine on his forehead. The stone sank into his forehead, and he fell face down to the ground. David defeated the Philistine with a sling and a stone.

— 1 Samuel 17:43-50

You should expect negativity when dealing with your giants. At times, you may be faced with embarrassing comments from others. You may have thoughts like, "I am not worthy enough." However, with God's direction, it is up to you push aside these thoughts and doubts. Be a representative of God through His strength and wisdom. God will and can handle all things that matter. Don't resist God's plan for your life. The body of Christ lives within us, and He is not going to ignore our cries for help! Let go of trying to take matters into your own hands and allow God to fight your battles. That's how much God loves you and me — enough to fight our battles for us!

God loves you, and this is His wish for you.

Dr. Charles Stanley – Sermon Notes – March 8, 2020 – THE PRICE OF POPULARITY

Do you find yourself jealous when others seem to be getting ahead? Did someone else get the promotion? Did someone else receive a financial blessing? Did someone else become blessed with a perfect family? Did someone else become blessed with an outstanding husband or wife?

There is a high price to pay for popularity, Dr. Stanley says, especially if you abuse that blessing. Popularity is a gift from God, and it is your responsibility to use it wisely. It is critical to always show humbleness when blessed with popularity. If you have received this blessing from God, you must understand the proper and intelligent way to handle it. Some may feel gaining popularity will bring a certain level of satisfaction. On the other hand, some may think this popularity is emptiness filled with broken promises. Some people do not even know they are popular. With popularity, you must learn to deal with anger, suspicion, and vengeance.

Where does the problem with jealousy arise? It is anger. Dr. Stanley says it breaks his heart to see Christian men and women who are jealous of each other. We become suspicious of others who have been blessed with popularity. We find ourselves engaged with everything that person does. We suspect them to be up to something that is not right.

Then there is vengeance, which can cause harm to others if it gets out of hand. Please, do not let this happen. Be the adult you need to be always and act appropriately. You are to be supportive of a person who is jealous without thoughts of vengeance. Always refuse to take revenge on any jealous person. Always show respect and humbleness. Be very careful about how you respond to a jealous person. Our job is to love and emotionally support them. For further learning on anger, suspicion, vengeance, and revenge, you can read the complete book of 1 Samuel.

Dr. Stanley tells the story of King David, who was once an unknown shepherd boy. Later in David's life, God gave him the blessing to be the King of Israel, and David immediately became the hero of Israel. As a young child, God knew David's heart, and God was preparing and prepping him for greatness all along. David's attribute was a heart with no jealousy.

An individual blessed with popularity may be taken advantage of. In some cases, you become their person to lean. Be on guard when people only want to hang around you because of your popularity. This type of behavior may be a fake friendship. Encourage them to develop a deeper relationship with our Lord Jesus Christ, encourage them to seek what God's plan is for them in their life.

We are God's children. He loves us and has the best plan for you and me. God tells us to wait and lean on Him. Yes, we are to lean on God and not rely on the popularity of others. God may take away the popularity He has granted you at any moment. You should show respect and humbleness at all times for one of God's precious gifts — the wisdom of understanding the real meaning of popularity.

God loves you, and this is His wish for you.

Dr. Charles Stanley – Sermon Notes – March 15, 2020 – TRUE GENUINE FRIENDSHIP

Definition of Friendship — the state of being friends; friendly feeling

Definition of Love — strong affection or liking of someone or something; a passionate affection of one person for another; the object of such affection; a sweetheart or lover; to woo, embrace

Definition of Emotion — to move; strong feeling; any specific feeling, such as love, hate, fear, or anger

Definition of Respect — to feel or show honor or esteem; to show consideration for; honor or esteem; consideration or regard; expression of reward; a particular detail; reference relation; respectful; respectfully

Definition of Mutual — to exchange, done, felt, etc. by each of two or more for or toward the other or others; of each other; in common our mutual friend; mutually

What kind of person draws you in? What is the quality of that individual which attracts you? What type of character do they possess? When you think about true friendship, these are some of the questions that you must ask yourself. It's very healthy to be drawn to a person that motivates you. It's perhaps the best emotional feeling you can obtain, because you become challenged to move out of your comfort zone. Finding a true friendship requires you to be a friend first. The first step in growing a friendship is to learn to love yourself and develop a sense of security within yourself. You then must learn to love another person more than you love yourself. This is a genuine friendship.

> *When David had finished speaking with Saul, Jonathan committed himself to David, and loved him as much as he loved himself. Saul kept David with him from that day on and did not let him return to his father's house. Jonathan made a covenant with David because he loved him as much as himself. Then Jonathan removed the robe he was wearing and gave it to David, along with his military tunic, his sword, his bow, and his belt.*
> — 1 Samuel 18:1-4

The three qualities of genuine friendship are:

- **Respect** — you cannot love someone if you do not respect them.
- **Emotion** — you must show strong feelings for that person, such as love and understanding.
- **Mutuality** — you must have a commonality with that individual and experience the same feelings. It must be a true understanding.

There is no cheap friendship. True friendship is expensive.

Jesus respects you and me and has expressed his love for us. Thank God each day for your true friendships. Listen when God speaks of respect, emotion, and mutuality. When doing so, you are pouring out our friendship with someone else. This is how much God loves us. With two people, one must show friendship first. Always remember in your heart, Jesus is man's greatest friend.

God loves you, and this is His wish for you.

53

Dr. Charles Stanley – Sermon Notes – March 22, 2020 – A COVENANT RELATIONSHIP

Definition of Covenant — an agreement, compact; to promise by a covenant; to make a covenant

When you hear words like trust, loyalty, eternal, responsibility, faithfulness, honesty, commitment, promise, agreement, devotion, eagerness, binding, arrangement, enduring, and love, what comes to your mind? Back in the old days, Dr. Stanley says, when two men shook hands on an agreement, it was a done deal. It was a genuine way to show you would keep your end of the bargain. Unfortunately, in the world we live in today, the word covenant has a different meaning. To illustrate the Biblical concept of covenant, please read both 1 Samuel and 2 Samuel. It talks about Jonathan and David, their commitment to one another, and their commitment to their families. It was a covenant sealed with blood and a handshake. It was an eternal covenant to each other. Today's covenant might be called "fake brotherhood."

In the story of Noah's Ark, God made a promise to Noah to never again flood the land with forty days and forty nights of rain. God kept his promise to Noah by creating the rainbow. Each time you see a rainbow, you are witnessing God's and Noah's covenant to each other.

There are four characteristics of a covenant: conditional, unconditional, temporary, and contract. A covenant is genuine loyalty and a form of protection to one and another. Dr. Stanley encourages everyone to know the importance and realize the meaning of the covenant.

Experience the greatest blessing of all. Allow God to come into your life and make a covenant with you. Repent and confess your sins. Acknowledge you believe God's son, the Lord Jesus Christ, paid for all your sins, so you may spend eternity with Him in Heaven. This is the most critical decision you will have to make in your life, Dr. Stanley says.

Today or tonight, ask yourself if you want to receive the Devil at death, or receive God's blessing of eternal life with your Heavenly Father. God is offering His unconditional love to you. God says, "Come as you are." You don't have to impress God because he already knows your inner heart. When you accept the Lord Jesus Christ as your savior, you immediately become a child of God.

Think about it before it's too late to make your covenant with God. Only a fool would choose the Devil.

God loves you, and this is His wish for you.

54

Dr. Charles Stanley – Sermon Notes – March 29, 2020 - WHAT IS GOD UP TO IN YOUR LIFE?

Be thankful to God always, no matter what you are encountering in your life. Rest assured, God has promised to be with you every step and every moment of the day. Understanding the proper way to pray is very helpful in difficult times. There may be times when the valley is too deep, and the fire is too hot. Be gentle with your prayers to God. Instead of asking Him to get me out of the fire, pray for God to walk through the fire with you. God teaches us to trust and lean on Him. You must realize that your strength and salvation are found in Him. God allows difficulties in your life because He is testing your perseverance. He wants to see how you handle issues when the bottom drops out of your life. Are you going to do things your way or God's?

Whatever God chooses, it is for your good and His glory. God has a way of sniffing you out for future greatness and services. He is also evaluating your weaknesses. Through all of this, God prepares the right "recipe" for your life. When God is sniffing you out, He is blessing someone else. God most definitely is in the sniffing and blessing business. God is still and silent during your times of trouble. He is checking your performance under pressure and evaluating your perseverance at the same time. God will do this to bring out the best qualities you possess.

With the Lord Jesus Christ living in you, you cannot sink. God is always close by, and you are under His wings and not held back in the shadow. Do not dishonor God by going around weeping and moaning. Allow God to oversee your circumstances. God reveals your weaknesses to wake you up. All He wishes is that you recognize your behavior in life, as well as what is causing these problems in the first place. This is all part of God's recycling process. He wants to see how you react when the pressure gets too intense and stares you in the face.

Dr. Stanley suggests reading about King David in the books 1 Samuel and 2 Samuel, which illustrate how God is prepping you and me, just as He did King David. God will reveal your weaknesses to you. When you respond properly, you are telling God how much you need Him. You also confess that you understand during times of trial and tribulations, God is building your character. Please, do not tamper with God's decisions. He loves you so much that He is working on the right recipe for you.

God loves you, and this is His wish for you.

55

Dr. Charles Stanley – Sermon Notes – April 5, 2020 — THE INSPIRATIONAL MESSAGE OF THE RESURRECTION

What does the resurrection mean to us?

On the first day of the week, very early in the morning, they came to the tomb, bringing the spices they had prepared. They found the stone rolled away from the tomb. They went in but did not find the body of the Lord Jesus. While they were perplexed about this, suddenly two men stood by them in dazzling clothes. So, the women were terrified and bowed down to the ground. "Why are you looking for the living among the dead?" asked the men.

"He is not here, but He has been resurrected! Remember how He spoke to you when He was still in Galilee, saying, 'The Son of Man must be betrayed into the hands of sinful men, be crucified, and rise on the third day'?" And they remembered His words.

Returning from the tomb, they reported all these things to the Eleven and to all the rest. Mary Magdalene, Joanna, Mary the mother of James, and the other women with them were telling the apostles these things. But these words seemed like nonsense to them, and they did not believe the women. Peter, however, got up and ran to the tomb. When he stooped to look in, he saw only the linen cloths. So, he went home, amazed at what had happened.

– Luke 24:1-12

As a believer, is Jesus Christ at the center of your life? Jesus Christ is the light of the world; He is the door; and He is the good shepherd. No one comes to the heavenly Father but through Jesus Christ! Do you talk to others about the resurrection, and what an impact it has made on your life? The resurrection is the most profound event that ever happened. That's how important this inspirational message is. This is the real reason why we celebrate Easter Sunday. Our Lord Jesus Christ has risen from the grave. Life is all about Jesus Christ. Your job is to believe, trust, obey, serve, share, and tell the world about Him. Jesus Christ is risen from the death. He is alive! He is risen and is seated at the right hand of our Heavenly Father. He lives within us, He has forgiven us, He is the ruler, He is our keeper, and He keeps his promises. He did all of this so one day we may spend eternal life in Heaven with Him. He is the Father, Son, and Holy Spirit.

When you become saved, it is not temporary. You are saved forever! God pardons our sins forever. He is dependable. God's desire is for us to live a clean life. What God says, He means. He says we shall never perish but have eternal life. He tells us that faith is greater than all. He speaks of eternal life; He speaks of security. God tells us no one can separate us from our Heavenly Father. He speaks of reassurance. We are His forgiven children, and the seal of the Holy Spirit cannot be broken. The Holy Spirit is a down payment, which means you belong to Him. God makes no mistakes!

Death is not the end of a believer! "For God so loved the world." If Jesus Christ is not the center of your life, and you're still doing things your way, ask the Lord Jesus to come into your life! Repent, confess your sins, surrender your life over to Him, believe our Lord Jesus Christ died on the cross at Calvary. Please do not miss out on God's greatest gifts — life and eternity.

God loves you, and this is His wish for you.

**Dr. Charles Stanley – Sermon Notes – April 12, 2020
– THE RESURRECTION MORNING**

On the first day of the week, very early in the morning, they came to the tomb, bringing the spices they had prepared. They found the stone rolled away from the tomb. They went in but did not find the body of the Lord Jesus. While they were perplexed about this, suddenly two men stood by them in dazzling clothes.

So, the women were terrified and bowed down to the ground. "Why are you looking for the living among the dead?" asked the men. "He is not here, but He has been resurrected! Remember how He spoke to you when He was still in Galilee, saying, 'The Son of Man must be betrayed into the hands of sinful men, be crucified, and rise on the third day'?"

And they remembered His words.

Returning from the tomb, they reported all these things to the Eleven and to all the rest. Mary Magdalene, Joanna, Mary the mother of James, and the other women with them were telling the apostles these things. But these words seemed like nonsense to them, and they did not believe the women. Peter, however, got up and ran to the tomb. When he stooped to look in, he saw only the linen cloths. So, he went home, amazed at what had happened.

– Luke 24:1-12

God loves you, and this is His wish for you.

57

Dr. Charles Stanley – Sermon Notes – April 13, 2020 – THE RESURRECTION

Praise the Lord He has risen. What is your first thought when you hear these words? Is it resurrection and eternity? Resurrection means risen and alive, Dr, Stanley says, whereas eternity is everlasting, and we shall not perish but have eternal life with our Heavenly Father. What spiritual impact has the resurrection made in your life? Is Jesus Christ the center of your life or is it you? Are you still trying to do things your way instead of trusting, relying, and leaning on Jesus Christ?

> *"I assure you: Anyone who hears My word and believes Him who sent Me has eternal life and will not come under judgment but has passed from death to life. I assure you: An hour is coming, and is now here, when the dead will hear the voice of the Son of God, and those who hear will live. For just as the Father has life in Himself, so also, He has granted to the Son to have life in Himself. And He has granted Him the right to pass judgment, because He is the Son of Man. Do not be amazed at this, because a time is coming when all who are in the graves will hear His voice and come out-those who have done good things, to the resurrection of life, but those who have done wicked things, to the resurrection of judgment. I can do nothing on My own. I judge only as I hear, and My judgment is righteous, because I do not seek My own will, but the will of Him who sent Me.*
> *– John 5:24-30*

About the times and the seasons: brothers, you do not need anything to be written to you. For you yourselves know very well that the Day of the Lord will come just like a thief in the night.

— 1 Thessalonians 5:1-2

We do not want you to be uninformed, brothers, concerning those who are asleep, so that you will not grieve like the rest, who have no hope. Since we believe that Jesus died and rose again, in the same way God will bring with Him those who have fallen asleep through Jesus. For we say this to you by a revelation from the Lord: We who are still alive at the Lord's coming will certainly have no advantage over those who have fallen asleep. For the Lord Himself will descend from heaven with a shout, with the archangel's voice, and with the trumpet of God, and the dead in Christ will rise first. Then we who are still alive will be caught up together with them in the clouds to meet the Lord in the air; and so, we will always be with the Lord. Therefore encourage one another with these words.

— 1 Thessalonians 4:13-18

You may be wondering what we will look like in heaven. Our bodies will have an exchange if you will and turned into glorified bodies filled with mercy and grace, just like our Heavenly Father. How will you adjust to the heavenly kingdom? It won't matter because we will all have glorified bodies, Dr. Stanley tells us, and we will all be doing the same thing. Interestingly enough, it is like what we are doing here on earth but only now in the presence of God FOREVER. We will serve and reign just like our heavenly father. We will all become part of God's big family.

*Now if Christ is in you, the body is dead because of sin,
but the Spirit gives life because of righteousness. And if
the Spirit of him who raised Jesus from the dead lives in
you, then he who raised Christ from the dead will also
bring your mortal bodies to life through his Spirit who
lives in you.*

— Romans 8:10:11

The Holy Spirit is your seal. It is God's down payment, "He belongs to me, she belongs to me." It is a seal that can never be broken. Once you are a Child of God, your seal becomes concrete. God does not perform partially. He is complete in all tasks, He makes no mistakes, and He is perfect. There is not one person or thing that can separate you from our Lord Jesus Christ. Once you become saved and a Child of God, it is a done deal.

*"Truly I tell you, unless someone is born again, he
cannot see the kingdom of God." "How can anyone be
born when he is old?" Nicodemus asked him, "can he
enter his mother's womb a second time and be formed?"
Jesus answered, "Truly I tell you unless someone is born
of water and the Spirit, he cannot enter the kingdom
of God. Whatever is born of the flesh is flesh, and
whatever is born of the Spirit is spirit. Do not be amazed
that I told you that you must be born again. The wind
blows where it pleases, and you hear its sound, but you
don't know where it comes from or where it is going. So,
it is with everyone born in the Spirit."*

— John 3:3-8

We are earthly creatures, and there are limitations to our understanding fully the most significant event to happen in the Bible — the resurrection and eternity. Have you ever thought about what your first words to God are going to be? Make your first words to God one of praise, "Thank you, thank you, dear Heavenly Father, for now, I have come home to you."

God loves you, and this is His wish for you.

58

**Dr. Charles Stanley – Sermon Notes –
April 19, 2020 — PURSUING GOD'S WILL
– HOW TO ENCOURAGE YOURSELF**

Definition of Tide — a period, now only in combination; the alternate rise, and fall, about twice a day, of the surface of oceans, seas, caused by the attraction of the moon and sun; something that rises and falls like the tide

Definition of Turbulent — wild or disorderly; full of violent motion

Definition of Intervene — to come or between; to occur between two events; to come between; to modify, to settle, or hinder some action

Today, are you standing in a disaster? Have you hit rock bottom? If the answer to these two questions is yes, then it is Satan that is orchestrating your life! Satan has flooded your thoughts with fear, doubt, despair, and brokenness! Do not allow Satan to attack you right in your rib cage.

To become the King of Israel, God had to break David down. God will break a person down to build them back up, like the rise and fall as in the ocean tide. God will never give up on His will of pursuing, therefore, you must think about our self-will vs. God's will.

How do you encourage yourself? You must reject the thoughts of fear and doubt, redirect the way you think, recall all the blessings the Lord has given, and review what kind of spirit is in your heart.

Ask yourself this question, "What is my mindset when it comes to emotional vs. reasoned thinking?" God desires to pour out His love in rock-bottom times. God is redirecting us to have a new beginning in life. God wants us to think the way He thinks and feel the encouragement of His will and not ours.

When the tide becomes too high, this means God is evaluating and illustrating the right way for you to face up to what you did to cause this mess in the first place. Use the tools to help evaluate the situation: reject, redirect, recall and review what is going on in your life. Once this has been analyzed, God will change the tide. Allow God to restore calmness in your life and rid it of turbulence. It is only through our Lord Jesus Christ that calmness will and can be restored. Please note what is stated in the Bible — God may use others to help intervene in this process.

What is the tide like in your life? Do you desire a new beginning? Do you desire to think like God? Do you desire calmness over turbulence? Face up to what is causing this turbulence. God has the best plan for us. Our job is to reject, redirect, recall and review. God loves us so much and created this perfect blueprint for our lives.

God loves you, and this is His wish for you.

Dr. Charles Stanley – Sermon Notes – April 26, 2020 - PURSUING GOD'S HEART – STAYING BY THE SUB – MUNDANE TASKS

Definition of Sub – under (submarine), lower than (subhuman)

Definition of Mundane – of the world, worldly, commonplace, ordinary

Definition of Profound – marked by intellectual depth, deeply felt, thorough-going

Now that you are saved and a believer in our Lord Jesus Christ, what you are doing to serve Him?

Ask yourself these questions: Am I doing my very best in the place God has put me? Am I answering God's call when He speaks?

Please, read 1 Samuel 30, David's Defeat of the Amalekites, which is the story of how David, in unprecedented times, found strength in the Lord. David is answering His calling. This passage will help you understand how to answer God when He calls you.

People performing "mundane" tasks are just as important as other people performing "important" tasks, and in some cases, even more so. There are six principles that apply to this theory:

1. Mundane things matter.
2. Stay the course and recognize there are certain qualities about the people doing tasks behind the scenes.
3. Recognize that these people are faithful servants of God.

4. Realize they may be performing these tasks because the situation is beyond their control.
5. Recognize that mundane tasks might be misunderstood by others and cause them to judge or cast aspersion on the person performing them.
6. God has ways of rewarding us when we "stay by the sub."

As children of God, we are all essential. God loves the person who does their very best, and He loves faithful performers. It is God who will judge you in your final hour, and if you have been someone instructed to do little things, those little things become big things in the eyes of our Lord Jesus Christ. Someday, you will have to make an account of your life. God will look at how truthful you were, the opportunities you were presented, and what you did with those opportunities. Do not misunderstand God when He has presented you with a "mundane" task. He may be only giving you a temporary task, so do your very best, be content, and set an example for others.

Ask yourself, "Am I doing my best where God has placed me?"

God loves you, and this is His wish for you.

**Dr. Charles Stanley – Sermon Notes – May 3, 2020 -
PURSUING GOD'S HEART – THE WORD OF GOD**

In this sermon, Dr. Stanley refreshed our minds about the Word of God. If it's not His words, then you are on the wrong path and not pursuing God's heart. Beware of curiosity, mediums, satanists, witchcraft, and deceivers.

It is normal to be curious, Dr. Stanley says, however, curiosity can lead to trouble if you don't recognize the consequences and boundaries of curiosity. True Christians are curious about the welfare of others. Parents, of course, are curious about what their children are doing, and all of this is a normal emotion. Parents must be watchful of their children. It is the responsibility of the parents to oversee what kind of movies their children are watching, what their children are listening to, what their children are reading, and more.

The devil will use colors and covers to be deceitful. Do not become fooled by the devil's methods of luring. Any other religions and theories other than our Heavenly Father's, our Lord Jesus Christ's, and the Bible should be discarded. If it is not the Spirit of God and the Spirit of God's heart, then it's nothing more than pure demonic and satanic thinking. We are children of God, and we have, by the grace of God, been sanctified. Thinking any other way may have dangerous consequences. Satan is a destroyer and will send demons to do your speaking for you. Beware of these possibilities.

Now the Spirit explicitly says that in the latter times some will depart from the faith, paying attention to deceitful spirits and the teachings of demons, through the hypocrisy of liars whose consciences are seared. They forbid marriage and demand abstinence from foods that God created to be received with gratitude by those who believe and know the truth. For everything created by God is good, and nothing should be rejected if it is received with thanksgiving, since it is sanctified by the word of God and by prayer.

— 1 Timothy 4:1-5

Honor God, praise Him, and recognize the right way to pursue God's heart is through His Word.

God loves you, and this is His wish for you.

**Dr. Charles Stanley – Sermon Notes – May 10, 2020
– THE TRUE TEST OF CHARACTER**

How a person responds in a time of crisis is the truest test of their character. It's important to understand that a minor crisis is just as real as a major one.

The best description of a man's character can be found in 1 Samuel and 2 Samuel, which both cover the life of King David.

David showed who he was by being a king of forgiveness. David was very cautious in following the ways of God, had great respect for gifted men, and was a man of prayer. David listened when God spoke, was consistent with every turn in his life, and was a man of loyalty. Lastly, David never forgot others. David set the perfect example by operating under the powers of steel and velvet, using both forces at the same time.

What do you do when power and prestige come your way? Dr. Stanley asks. Are you able to handle these gifts? Only God knows your heart, how you feel, and how you conduct yourself in times of power and crisis. You must learn to always lean on God. In all circumstances, you must turn to God first and ask Him what to do.

You must remember there is a right and a wrong way of doing things. There will be times in your life when you experience a lapse in judgment. Dr. Stanley says this is very normal. Before you judge yourself too quickly, you must look beyond actions and look to your heart.

Today, be thankful and praise God for changing your character to be one pleasing to Him.

God loves you, and this is His wish for you.

Dr. Charles Stanley – Sermon Notes – May 17, 2020 – PURSUING GOD'S HEART – OPEN AND HONEST

Today, be thankful God will send you a helper — the Holy Spirit, who dwells within you to purify your heart. The Holy Spirit has the authority and the power to cleanse your heart.

Is your heart right with God? Dr. Stanley says for God to work in your life effectively, your heart must be purified. When you speak to God do you mean business? We all are waiting and looking for the right answers to our prayers. When you reach the point where God has not answered your prayers, it is because your heart has not been purified.

God desires for you to be bold and honest sitting before Him. Here are some ways you can expect to respond to God: reflections on your past; recalling what God is like, including His greatness, goodness, His grace, and where He has brought you from; remembering God's promises and, finally, making your request. God always wants to speak to you personally. A new picture of your life will start to unfold. Did you know God is in the healing business and will always keep his promise if you do your part?

God wants you to be everything He has created you to be. He has the right blueprint for your life. Are you willing to sit down with God and be open and honest? Do you want to reach out to God with a clean heart? God is waiting for you with open arms when you pursue a lifestyle pleasing to him.

God loves you, and this is His wish for you.

Dr. Charles Stanley – Sermon Notes – May 24, 2020 – SITTING BEFORE GOD AND THE SEVEN NECESSITIES

In today's busy world, there are so many distractions. When you sit before the Lord, a thousand thoughts might be rushing through your mind, making it impossible to listen to God when He speaks. Dr. Stanley says this is all about the mystery of God.

Are you willing to wait for God's perspective? Could it be God wants you to stop doing what you have been doing and give some time to Him? Do not let the devil do the speaking for you. When your mind starts to drift, it is the work of the devil, not God.

Dr. Stanley outlines the seven necessities of sitting before God:

1. season-time
2. stillness
3. seclusion
4. silence
5. self-control
6. sensitivity
7. submissive spirit

It is up to you to pick a time to sit before God. Wasting time is an act created by the devil, so find a special location and time to start worshiping God. You are on the right path when you hear God's voice. Be keen when God speaks to you.

You will find what you're looking for when God replies to you. Seal it in your heart and establish it in your thinking. Allow God to teach you the right way to deal with conflict by replacing it with peace.

Daily, become more like our Lord Jesus Christ in every way. Walk in His path and in His light instead of darkness. Use your empowerment and mind by these seven necessities when sitting before God.

God loves you, and this is His wish for you.

Dr. Charles Stanley – Sermon Notes – June 7, 2020 - PURSUING GOD'S HEART – A MOMENTS OF WEAKNESS

Definition of Defense – a defense against attack; something that defends; justification by speech or writing; the arguments of a defendant, the defendant, and his or her counsel

Definition of Defense Mechanism – any thought process used unconsciously to protect oneself against painful feelings

Definition of Weakness – state of being weak; a weak point; an immoderate fondness (for something)

Definition of Bout – a struggle or contest; a period of some activity

Definition of Abandon – to give up completely; unrestrained activity

Definition of Theology – the study of God and religious doctrines and matters of divinity

We all, at some time or another, have had moments of weakness. Did you know that weakness brushes out your ability to get what you want? This means you are brushing out God and giving permission for Satan to divide your mind. This is why understanding the meaning and consequences of weakness are so very important. What are the lasting consequences of weakness?

Dr. Stanley suggests reading 2 Samuel 11, David's Adultery with Bathsheba, which shows King David and his struggles with weakness. There are seven ways to build a defense against weakness, Dr. Stanley teaches.

1. acknowledge the reality of your weakness
2. analyze the pattern and identify the pattern
3. anticipate the moments so you're not caught off guard
4. accurately identify these exact weakness and check the timing
5. awareness of your accountability to God
6. abandon and throw it all overboard
7. allow extra time for God in prayer and meditation

God uses weakness for greater potential. He already knows your potential and He knows how wise and positive you are. During times of weakness, God will say, "Stop! I will use your potential instead."

Allow God to work in your heart and flush out your weaknesses. In doing so, God builds you up with courage, confidence, and strength. When dealing with weakness, do not say, "I think" but instead say, "I know." This is the right way to handle weakness. Do not encourage moments of weakness just to get what you want. It is always better to live your life under the umbrella of accountability to God and no one else.

God loves you, and this is His wish for you.

Dr. Charles Stanley – Sermon Notes – June 14, 2020 -
PURSUING GOD'S HEART – HOW TO RESPOND TO SIN

Definition of Repent – to feel such regret over an action, intention, etc. as to change one's mind (about); repentance

Definition of Forgive – to give up resentment against or the desire to punish; pardon (an offense or offender) to cancel

Definition of Sin – the willful breaking of the religious or moral law; any offense or fault; to commit a sin

Definition of Abandon – to put under; to give up completely; to the desert; abandonment

Definition of Rebellion – armed resistance to one's government; a defense of any authority

No matter what condition your heart is in, God is always right there with you. God has promised never to abandon you. It is also important to know that when you sin, you are breaking God's heart. When you sin, you are responding to the ways of Satan, not to the ways of God. Dr. Stanley says no one is above sinning. Through our failures, God will instruct us to deal with our sins so we may be more useful to Him. Sin is covered in 2 Samuel 11, David's Adultery with Bathsheba.

> Be gracious to me, God, according to Your faithful love; according to Your abundant compassion, blot out my rebellion. Wash away my guilt, and cleanse me from my sin. For I am conscious of my rebellion, and my

sin is always before me. Against You-You alone-I have sinned and done this evil in Your sight. So You are right when You pass sentence; You are blameless when You judge. Indeed, I was guilty [when I] was born; I was sinful when my mother conceived me. Surely You desire integrity in the inner self, and You teach me wisdom deep within. Purify me with hyssop, and I will be clean; wash me, and I will be whiter than snow. Let me hear joy and gladness; let the bones You have crushed rejoice. Turn Your face away from my sins and blot out all my guilt. God, create a clean heart for me and renew a steadfast spirit within me.

— Psalms 51:1-10

Reading these scriptures offers peacefulness when we sit before God. We can be just like King David and say these same words of wisdom.

The best way to deal with your sins is to repent, admit you have sinned against God, and accept full responsibility for our sins. You must be open and honest with God and then accept His loving forgiveness.

God desires for you to live in harmony, peacefulness, and happiness. Allow God to wash away all your sins and blot out all rebellion, guilt, and grieving. Our responsibility, no matter what, is to reject sin. God is waiting when we repent to send His forgiveness.

God loves you, and this is His wish for you.

66

Dr. Charles Stanley – Sermon Notes – June 21, 2020 –
PURSUING GOD'S HEART – RESPOND TO SIN

Definition of Fail – to be insufficient, fall short; to weaken, die away; to stop operating; to be negligent in duty, expectation, etc.; to be unsuccessful; to become bankrupt; to get a grade of failure; to be of no help; to disappoint; to be abandoned; to neglect

Why do we yield to temptation? What is it we have never been taught that draws us to sin? Did you know when you sin, you are sinning against God? You are not only hurting yourself but hurting God, as well. Dr. Stanley reminds us it is critical to stay in the Word of God during times of temptation. It is amazing what you can learn about God and how He operates. It is heartbreaking to ask God, "Why do I keep failing?"

In the fight against sin, God will instruct you to seek genuine repentance, to be willing to accept God's forgiveness, and to understand there will be discipline.

Discipline is an act of God's love. God is building you up as He deepens your relationship with him. God is always correcting you to become a better disciple, not only on your behalf but to share with others. Sharing your experiences with others is God's desire.

God will teach you humility, purification, and instructions. To ask God to un-mess, you must realize your responsibility and apply God's instructions. What are you going to do to change your sinful ways?

God does not want you to struggle alone with sin. Seeking professional help is always advised. It helps if you can find someone who has experienced sin and can be encouraging. Please, do not be too proud to ask for help. Admit you are in trouble, and you need help. Satan is always lurking around to defeat you. Satan will attempt to blind you when you seek counseling. Satan loves to frustrate. It is pleasing to God when we become wise and equip ourselves to fight against sin.

God loves you, and this is His wish for you.

**Dr. Charles Stanley – Sermon Notes – June 28, 2020
— CONTINUALLY CONSEQUENCES OF SIN**

Definition of Chastise – to punish, by beating; to scold sharply, chastisement

Definition of Chasten – to punish as to correct; to restrain or subdue

Definition of Continue – to last, endure; to go on in a specified course of action or condition; to extend; to stay; to go on again after an interruption; to go with; to extend; to cause to remain; to postpone

Definition of Consequence – a result, effect; important, take the consequences to accept the results of one's action

Definition of Mock – to ridicule; to mimic as in fun or derision; to express scorn; ridicule, sham, imitation, pretend, false or insincerely

God does not erase the consequences of sin. God will no longer hold you guilty, however, it is biblically written there will be continuing consequences for sinning. When you violate God's principles of sin, the results are very expensive. Sin is so powerful it can ruin an entire nation.

Do not think you can mock God and get away with it. God will track you down and stop you right in your tracks to expose your sins. God may retract completely from you. It is God's way of showing how much he loves you. This is a process known as the Act of God's Love, which draws you closer to our Heavenly Father.

> *Therefore since we also have such a large cloud of witnesses surrounding us, let us lay aside every weight and the sin that so easily ensnares us, and run with endurance the race that lies before us, keeping our eyes on Jesus, the source and perfecter of our faith, who for the joy that lay before Him endured a cross and despised the shame, and has sat down at the right hand of God's throne.*
> — Hebrews 12:1-2

God loves you, and this is His wish for you.

68

**Dr. Charles Stanley – Sermon Notes – July 5, 2020
– PURSUING GOD'S HEART CONTINUALLY
CONSEQUENCES OF OUR CONDUCT – SIN -**

Definition of Sin – the willful breaking of the religious or moral law, any offense or fault, to commit sin

Definition of Chastisement – to punish, by beating, to scold sharply, to correct, to restrain, or subdue

Definition of Consequences – a result, effect, take the consequences to accept the results of one's action

Definition of Aborning – while being born or created

Definition of Abortion – an expulsion of a fetus before it can survive, esp. if induced on purpose – abortionist

Definition of Abort – to have a miscarriage, to cause to have an abortion, to cut short

Definition of Abortive – unsuccessful; fruitless, arrested in development

Definition of Deceive – to make a person believe what is not true; mislead

Dr. Stanley's important warning and alert against sin. The best example of a violation of sin may be explained by reading the complete Scripture, 2 Samuel.

Do you think you can sin and get away with it? Allowing ourselves to think this way, we are mocking God. It is biblically written, there will be stricken consequences of sinning. God does not erase the consequences of our sin. God will no longer hold you guilty, however, it is biblically written, there will be continuing (never to go away), consequences of sinning. God will track you down and stop you right in your tracks to expose your sin. God will use His power of chastisement. Extremely important to note, sin is a violation of God's principles in lessons and challenges. When we continually commit acts of sin, we are breaking God's heart, we are breaking our hearts, and the hearts of others. Sin is a trap brought about by the work of the devil.

What is our responsibility for sin? We must turn to God with genuine repentance, and ask forgiveness. Forgiveness so that we may move forward into righteousness. Allow God to use His act of love in your life, even if it means His chastisement. God is always willing and ready to receive you just as you are with open arms.

God loves you, and this is His wish for you.

69

Dr. Charles Stanley – Sermon Notes – July 12, 2020
CONSEQUENCES OF SIN

Dr. Stanley's important sermon message against sin and the domino effect it will have in one's life is in 2 Samuel. There is no greater explanation in the Bible of how sin operates in a person's life. Sin is so powerful it can ruin an entire nation. Please, do not think you can mock God and get away with it. If you do, you are deceiving yourself. When you violate God's principles, there are consequences. Dr. Stanley is very clear how you will be held accountable. There is no way one can escape God's word or God's consequences for sin.

> *If we say, "We have no sin," we are deceiving ourselves, and the truth is not in us. If we confess our sins, He is faithful and righteous to forgive us our sins and to cleanse us from all unrighteousness.*
> — 1 John 1:8-9

Here are God's Five Principles of Continuing Consequences of Sin:

1. Continuing consequences of sin is a biblical principle that cannot be altered.
2. Continuing consequences of sin is an act of divine chastisement. God uses chastisement as a safeguard to future sin and to correct us.
3. There is no incomplete unfinished forgiveness of sin without consequences. Dr. Stanley says we will have to

suffer for our sins and live with the guilt we have brought upon ourselves to face the consequences.

4. For those who want to sin and think there will be no consequences, you are only deceiving yourself.

5. Continuing consequences of sin may be known only to the guilty one.

Sin will find you out, Dr. Stanley warns. There is absolutely no way you can hide or run away from sin. There is no isolation of sin with God. He will bring it out into the open. Dealing with sin the moment it occurs is the proper, mature response. Do not pretend nothing happened. Neglecting sin creates a domino effect so big that no one can stop it. It may even reach the point of deadliness.

Your goal is to be a faithful disciple. Think in terms of creating a relationship and fellowship with God. Understand the importance of God's love for you, and how He longs to bring obedience, peace, and harmony to everyone.

Allow God to cleanse your heart and rid it of any sin. All sin is equal in the eyes of God. There will always be guilt you must address and learn to deal with.

Every day of your life, you must strive to be more like God and live according to His principles. If you continue to sin and disobey God, it is guaranteed there will be strict consequences. They may be overflowing consequences, day after day, with no peace.

Please stop the devil from casting a spell of sin on you, which creates that domino effect.

God loves you, and this is His wish for you.

70

Dr. Charles Stanley – Sermon Notes – July 19, 2020 – MADE FOR THE MOUNTAINS

He makes my feet like [the feet of] a deer and sets me securely on the heights.

— 2 Samuel 22:34

Living the life of a Christian is sometimes not easy. However, when God created us, He made all of us climbers. Like the deer, God equipped you with ability to cling to the rock and keep moving upward, even when the fog becomes thick, and you cannot see. God had in mind for you to conduct your life like climber, always going upward, and not just wandering around living a life of ease on the Earth. God equipped you to be the best He wants you to be, to live as 'mountain climbers" and not live in the lowlands. Don't think, "Well, I work hard and will do what I want to live a life in leisure." God's goal is to always move you upward. With God, there is no swimming downstream, and you are to struggle upstream.

Reaching the peak of the mountain, you can see and appreciate the best view of everything. It is an opportunity to reflect and grow closer to God. On top of the peak, you get a better perspective on the direction of your life. It is an opportunity to be alone with God and meditate. It is a haven. Just like the deer, the higher you travel the safer you feel. The air is fresher, and you're in a position to shut out the world. It is God and you in your special time. Dr. Stanley teaches that the first preference in a person's life must be meditation. Once a person reaches a plateau, the next climb is on its way, which may be easier or harder. There may be times when

God places a cloud in your way because He wants to see how you react. Will you lean and trust in God, or will you do things your way? God wants you to find your potential. He wants to know the condition of your heart and your mindset. God wants to know if you are on the right track. God wants you to keep climbing mountains until the time He calls you home.

Just like a pilot flying an airplane alone, Dr. Stanley says, meditation is being blessed with solitude, experiencing the first and foremost important preference in life.

Cherish how God created you to be like the deer who clings to the rocks. Honor and show God your potential in life by climbing every mountain. Ask yourself this question, "Am I made for the mountains?"

God loves you, and this is His wish for you.

**Dr. Charles Stanley – Sermon Notes – July 26, 2020
– A MAN AFTER GOD'S OWN HEART**

Do you hunger or desire to be a man or woman after God's own heart? King David did.

> *After removing him, He raised up David as their king, of whom He testified: 'I have found David the son of Jesse, a man after My heart, who will carry out all My will.'*
> — Acts 13:22

> *I have found David My servant; I have anointed him with My sacred oil. My hand will always be with him, and My arm will strengthen him. The enemy will not afflict him; no wicked man will oppress him. I will crush his foes before him and strike those who hate him. My faithfulness and love will be with him, and through My name his horn will be exalted. I will extend his power to the sea and his right hand to the rivers. He will call to Me, 'You are my Father, my God, the rock of my salvation.' I will also make him My firstborn, greatest of the kings of the earth. I will always preserve My faithful love for him, and My covenant with him will endure. I will establish his line forever, his throne as long as heaven lasts.*
> — Psalms 89:20-29.

As a small boy, while meditating and attending to his sheep, David saw God's blueprint and footprint right before his very own eyes. He desired to become a man after God's own heart. Dr. Stanley mentions four qualities of a person after God's own heart — prioritize a personal relationship, a strong desire for obedience to God, faith in God when things get tough, and become a servant.

A person after God's own heart carries a certain distinction. They are recognized by a certain kind of spirit. They know they are not perfect, and they are the first to admit disobedience and avoid placing blame on others. They take ownership of their disobedience. A person after God's own heart is always setting a higher goal for themselves. They know the responsibility and consequences of disobedient action. They do not run and hide or act childish. Acting childish in a broken world is not acceptable to God, and there will be chastisement. You can't run and hide from God because He will find you. You must be truthful. God already knows what happened.

Becoming a rebellious person is not what God desires for you. Instead, turn away from unacceptable behavior to become a better servant. That is exactly what King David did. In the battle between David and the Giant, David knew he had drawn on his strength and faith by relying on God. David saw God's blueprint and footprint right before his very own eyes. David knew he wanted to be a man after God's own heart and won the battle with a sling and rock. You can win your battle if you prioritize your relationship with God. Be strong and obedient, have faith, and be a better servant. These commands are small compared to eternal life with our Lord Jesus Christ.

God loves you, and this is His wish for you.

**Dr. Charles Stanley – Sermon Notes – August
2, 2020 – SEVING GOD'S PURPOSE**

You we were born to serve and worship our Lord Jesus Christ. Are you working for this? What is it that motivates you? What are you living for? If you are not serving or worshiping, Dr. Stanley says, then you are missing out on one of the greatest opportunities of being a servant to our Lord Jesus Christ. It is never too late to start serving, worshiping, and preparing. God is fully aware of what you have or have not done when He calls us home.

> *For David, after serving God's purpose in his generation,*
> *fell asleep was buried with his fathers, and decayed.*
> — Acts 13:36

King David was not a perfect servant, but he never said, "No." to God.

Jesus did not come to be served. He came to be a servant for you, me, and others.

Dr. Stanley says it is easy to live on your very own island and protect your shores, but God has nothing to do with that. You are here now to love, serve, and avoid isolation.

Jesus was ignored by multiple people who thought of Him as a troublemaker. You must never think that you are less than serving. Why? Because that is what others thought about our Lord Jesus Christ when He served. You must think in terms of being the most significant servant, born to serve and worship.

Through God's grace and favor, He wants to serve people around you through you. God will never ask anything you cannot do. You may think, "God, this is a mistake. You must be speaking to someone else. I'm not going to do it." God allows these circumstances in the first place. Please, do not moan and groan when God presents a request. Think of the request as the most fantastic opportunity you'll ever have. Remember, God will never ask anything you cannot do.

Starting today, make your life count. Never belittle yourself as "just a..." but become the best servant that you possibly can. Remember, it is not in your work but your service to one another that counts.

How to serve in this current generation? Refuse to be a slave, refuse to run from injustice, discover your need, start where you are, prepare yourself for future opportunities, and prepare a way for others to follow you.

These scriptures will help you gain a better understanding:

> *The righteous thrive like a palm tree and grow like a cedar tree in Lebanon.*
> — Psalms 92:12

> *If anyone serves Me, he must follow Me. Where I am, there My servant also will be. If anyone serves Me, the Father will honor him.*
> — John 12:26

For God is not unjust; He will not forget your work and the love you showed for His name when you served the saints-and you continue to serve them.

— Hebrews 6:10

By God's grace and favor, He wants to serve people around you through you. Never turn down God when He calls upon you.

God loves you, and this is His wish for you.

73

Dr. Charles Stanley – Sermon Notes - August 9, 2020 - FORWARD BY FAITH

As a new Christian, there will be days when you may feel like you are moving backward, which Dr. Stanley says is normal. Did you know the Christian life is a walk in spirit, a walk in life, and a walk in truth? So, why can't you get ahead? It might be your genuine understanding of faith is incorrect. During these times of doubt, Dr. Stanley suggest, is when you must change gears.

A good example is when you are struggling with hardships and barriers, and witnessing family, friends, and co-workers going through the same. Day after day, you witness their existence and how they seem to rise above it all. They have a clear understanding of genuine faith and what it represents. This is how they move forward. It is having trust and courage in our Lord Jesus Christ. Our faith must not be moved by feelings nor sight but through God only. It is much easier to walk forward than backward.

How do you change gears to correct your faith?

> *Therefore, though we are always confident and know that while we are at home in the body we are away from the Lord — for we walk by faith, not by sight — yet we are confident and satisfied to be out of the body and at home with the Lord.*
> — 2 Corinthians 5:6–8

There are three main areas that represent genuine faith — assurance, anticipation, and awareness. Assurance means that you believe in and have confidence in God. Anticipation is moving to do something about it. With awareness, you begin to witness changes happening in your life.

Genuine faith quiets a person's spirit. Once you have made your request, you now can rest. Once you have put your faith and confidence in the hands of God, your work is done. It is now up to God to honor your request. When you start to understand genuine faith, you also understand the importance of appreciation. You begin to thank God more and ask of less of Him. God keeps His word, period. God does not ignore genuine faith.

When life becomes difficult, rely on God, and have the courage to change gears. A Christian life is a walk in spirit, life, and truth.

God loves you, and this is His wish for you.

**Dr. Charles Stanley – Sermon Notes – August 16,
2020 – FORWARD BY FAITH – Part 2**

Definition of Acid Test – a crucial, final test

Definition of Faith – unquestionable belief, specif. in God; a religion, etc.; a particular religion; complete trust or confidence; loyalty

Definition of Obey – to carry out the orders; to be guided by one's conscience; to be obedient

Definition of Insult — to subject to an act, remark, etc.; meant to hurt the feelings of pride; an insulting act, remark, etc.

> *...who by faith conquered kingdoms, administered justice, obtained promises, shut the mouths of lions, quenched the raging of fire, escaped the edge of the sword, gained strength after being weak, became mighty in battle, and put foreign armies to flight. Women received their dead raised to life again. Some men were tortured, not accepting release, so that they might gain a better resurrection, and others experienced mockings and scourgings, as well as bonds and imprisonment. They were stoned, they were sawed in two, they died by the sword, they wandered about in sheepskins, in goatskins, destitute, afflicted, and mistreated. The world was not worthy of them. They wandered in deserts, mountains, caves, and holes in the ground. All these were approved through their faith, but they did not receive what was*

promised, since God had provided something better for
us, so that they would not be made perfect without us.
— Hebrews 11:33-40

What represents genuine faith? Here are the seven main areas:

1. Assurance — this means you believe and have confidence in your request to God. It's having confidence in what you ask for and what God is going to bring.
2. Anticipation — you must start to prepare and make plans for your request. Dr. Stanley says this is a vital part of your faith to move toward achieving your goal.
3. Awareness — this part involves trust and listening to the Holy Spirit. God is already up to something. Believing what God is doing for you will result in a "done deal."
4. Access — allow God to give you the key to unlocking the "treasure house." God is waiting for you to walk in faith the correct way, so He will provide you the right key. This is achieved by placing your trust in the almighty Heavenly Father, our Lord Jesus Christ.
5. Authority — do not demand of God. When this happens, it is like putting an ant against an elephant, resulting in moving backward. Placing your trust in God is how we obtain our authority in God.
6. Action — the acid test of faith is in obedience. Disbelief in God is an insult to Him. Do not present God with disobedience in your life.
7. Approval — *I waited patiently for the Lord, and He turned to me and heard my cry for help He brought me up from a desolate pit, out of the muddy clay, and set my feet on a rock, making my steps secure He put a new song in my mouth, a hymn of praise to our God. Many will see and fear and put their trust in the Lord.* — Psalms 40

Walking in faith is not only for you but becomes a blessing to others. When people see what God is doing in your life, they will also learn to walk in faith. It truly is a blessing to witness the beauty of how this works. We help others by setting a spiritual example and moving in a forward direction. This is what makes God happy. Dr. Stanley asks, "What direction are you moving in? Does it include assurance, anticipation, awareness, access, authority, action, and approval?"

We are reminded that a Christian life is all about trusting and obeying our Lord Jesus Christ, as well as applying these amazing tools to accomplish this blissful quest. Walk in genuine faith. When this happens, there is no doubt or question that you are walking in the forward, and this makes God happy. Do not insult God by breaking his heart, disobeying, not trusting, or not believing, for God loves and wants only the very best for you.

God loves you, and this is His wish for you.

Dr. Charles Stanley – Sermon Notes – August 30, 2020 - THE CALL OF FAITH

God is always moving you forward. You are never alone when God calls you into the unknown because He already knows the outcome of His request. Please, do not miss out on God's opportunity for you — the call of faith. In some instances, God's call may be a test of your faith. Read Genesis 12, which Dr. Stanley recommends understanding Abraham. By reading this book you will understand God's, four principles of the call of faith:

Principle 1: A Step into the Unknown — this action requires you to trust in God to accomplish it. It may be unknown strange, dishonest, and looked down upon by family and friends. However, it is not unknown to God.

> *By faith Abraham, when he was called, obeyed and went out to a place he was going to receive as an inheritance; he went out, not knowing where he was going. By faith he stayed as a foreigner in the land of promise, living in tents with Isaac and Jacob, co-heirs of the same promise. For he was looking forward to the city that has foundations, whose architect and builder is God.*
> — Hebrews 11:8-10

Principle 2: A Call for Separation — during this time, our comfort zone is disrupted, resulting in our faith going to sleep. This is dangerous because now we have thoughts of taking circumstances into our own hands.

Principle 3: A Call of Promise and Blessing — one may experience blood, sweat, tears, and journeys through dark valleys. However, God will keep His promise of a blessing. Yes, we are to look beyond the hurt. God promises it gets better and better.

Principle 4: A Call of Faith — this involves tests and trials. It is true that sometimes God will test your faith. It is also true that God will place barriers between your desires and His blessings. If your request does not line up with God, then you are probably in trouble.

During these times, we start to manipulate, twist, and turn circumstances to go our way. Be open and honest when seeking God's advice. Allow God to be your number one confidant in all things you do. God is your leader; He is your Father and He loves you. God always has the best plan for you. In all decisions, ask Him, "What would you do, God"? Lastly, never be afraid to step out into the unknown, for God is with you every step of the way. Your job is to listen, believe, trust, and obey His commands. Please remember, God is always moving us forward and upward, so we may experience His promises and blessings.

God loves you, and this is His wish for you.

Dr. Charles Stanley – Sermon Notes – September 6, 2020 - FAITH'S FIXED FOCUS

If you want the very best God has to offer, you must understand the true principles of faith. In his sermon, Faith's Fixed Focus, Dr. Stanley illustrates the life of Joseph as a young man, which is explained in Genesis 37-50.

Joseph as a young man, probably about 17 years old, when he was sold into slavery by his brothers, wrongfully jailed, repeatedly forgotten, and rejected by his family. Joseph didn't know those obstacles were all part of God's great plan for the nation of Israel. Don't despair when hardship strikes. God is doing something great for you and His kingdom. Just stick to God's plan for your life. Parents, your children must learn to trust in God and to live each day and each moment in faith.

> *Consider it a great joy, my brothers, whenever you experience various trials,_knowing that the testing of your faith produces endurance. But endurance must do its complete work, so that you may be mature and complete, lacking nothing._Now if any of you lacks wisdom, he should ask God, who gives to all generously and without criticizing, and it will be given to him._But let him ask in faith without doubting. For the doubter is like the surging sea, driven and tossed by the wind._ That person should not expect to receive anything from the Lord. An indecisive man is unstable in all his ways.*
> *– James 1:2-8*

No one undergoing a trial should say, "I am being tempted by God." For God is not tempted by evil, and He Himself doesn't tempt anyone. But each person is tempted when he is drawn away and enticed by his own evil desires. Then after desire has conceived, it gives birth to sin, and when sin is fully grown, it gives birth to death.

— James 1:13-15

Dr. Stanley advises watching your attitude, standing with confidence, and keeping calm. Remember, God has put you into that circumstance to be the best you can be. Violating the principles of the scripture is unacceptable to God.

If you want the very best God has to offer, you must understand the true principles of faith. God will protect you just as he protected Joseph. Therefore, just stick to God's plan, and He will see you through.

God loves you, and this is His wish for you.

Dr. Charles Stanley – Sermon Notes – September 13, 2020 – FAITH'S FIXED FOCUS – Part 2

Definition of Sustain – to keep in existence; to carry the weight; to support; to endure, withstand; to comfort or encourage; to suffer; to uphold the validity of; to confirm, corroborate

Definition of Faith – unquestionable belief, specif. in God, a religion, a particular religion; complete trust or confidence; loyalty

Definition of Focus – to concentrate; an adjustment of this to make a clear image; any center activity attention; produce a clear image

Definition of Fixed – firmly in place, established, settled, resolute; unchanging, persistent

It is so easy to become distracted in today's world. Dr. Stanley encourages everyone to adopt "Faith, Fixed, Focus," and incorporate these three necessary Biblical ways into their everyday life.

You can move forward when bad things happen. You do not need to shut down nor be embarrassed. Through all barriers and all circumstances there is hope. Your responsibility is to direct your attention to faith, firmly fix your mind, and concentrate on a clear image of God's plan for a better life.

Genesis 39-41, The Life of Joseph, is the perfect example of "Faith, Fixed, Focus."

When Joseph was sold into slavery by his brothers, wrongfully jailed, and repeatedly forgotten, he did not know those obstacles were all part of God's great plan for the nation of Israel. So, don't despair when hardship strikes. God is doing something great for you and His kingdom. Just stick to God's plan for your life.

During Joseph's dark days, he became sustainable. Whatever happened to Joseph, he felt he was responsible for it. He carried the weight and did not waver. No matter what happened, the Lord was with him. Joseph did not let his environment define him. He fixed his faith on Jehovah. When you do that, along with trusting and not letting others push you aside, you will prosper. Our Heavenly Father is with you. Do not miss God's blessing and seek help from others. If you ask, "God where are you?" He will answer, "My ways are not your ways." Stick to God's plan for your life. As a believer, our "Faith, Fixed, Focus" is upon God and God only. Learn to trust in God when hardship strikes and remember that He always knows the right decision and the right path to take.

God loves you, and this is His wish for you.

Dr. Charles Stanley – Sermon Notes – September 20, 2020 – THE WAY OF FAITH

If you say to God, "I cannot stand this any longer," He will respond, "Just wait for a little longer. I have something bigger and better for you." God has a higher purpose, and His goal is always larger than ours. Living with the wisdom of God's faith is the only correct way. It entails having faith, trusting, believing, and obeying in His commands. This is how faith works. God's ways are different from our ways. However, there is hope when you walk in faith and have patience.

The first thing you must do is evaluate your faith. Do you fully understand there are two ways of living life: — walk in faith or doing things as you please. The second thing you must do is take a look at your assets, such your house, car, and career. Your number one asset must be faith, Dr. Stanley says. Faith must come first!

> *Now faith is the reality of what is hoped for, the proof of what is not seen. For by it our ancestors were approved. By faith we understand that the universe was created by the word of God, so that what is seen has been made from things that are not visible.*
> — Hebrews 11:1-3

It is not easy living by faith, Dr. Stanley tells us. There will be suffering, trials, obstacles, hardships, and disappointments. Your responsibility is to trust, believe, and obey God, as we walk our path of life. Sometimes, living life in faith may be the longest way, but always the right way with God.

You must be patient and remember God works and operates differently for everyone. Just when you say, "God, I cannot stand this any longer," God will respond, "Just wait for a little longer. I have something bigger and better for you."

God loves you, and this is His wish for you.

Dr. Charles Stanley – Sermon Notes – September 27, 2020 - THE WAY OF FAITH – Part 2

Sometimes the way of faith is the longest and most misunderstood way. Dr. Stanley talks about Moses, an ordinary man and sheepherder, who lived for 40 years in the desert. During this time, he struggled transitioning from murderer to humble man. However, it was during this time Moses maintained his abundant faith in God. This is what set him apart from others and empowered him to accomplish what seemed impossible.

Moses and the Burning Bush – His Battle against Pharaoh and the Parting of the Red Sea...

> *Then the Angel of the Lord appeared to him in a flame of fire within a bush. As Moses looked, he saw that the bush was on fire but was not consumed. So Moses thought: I must go over and look at this remarkable sight. Why isn't the bush burning up? When the Lord saw that he had gone over to look, God called out to him from the bush, "Moses, Moses!" "Here I am," he answered. "Do not come closer," He said. "Take your sandals off your feet, for the place where you are standing is holy ground."*
>
> *Then He continued, "I am the God of your father, the God of Abraham, the God of Isaac, and the God of Jacob." Moses hid his face because he was afraid to look at God. Then the Lord said, "I have observed the misery of My people in Egypt, and have heard them*

crying out because of their oppressors, and I know about their sufferings. I have come down to rescue them from the power of the Egyptians and to bring them from that land to a good and spacious land, a land flowing with milk and honey-the territory of the Canaanites, Hittites, Amorites, Perizzites, Hivites, and Jebusites.

The Israelites' cry for help has come to Me, and I have also seen the way the Egyptians are oppressing them. Therefore, go. I am sending you to Pharaoh so that you may lead My people, the Israelites, out of Egypt." But Moses asked God, "Who am I that I should go to Pharaoh and that I should bring the Israelites out of Egypt?" He answered, "I will certainly be with you, and this will be the sign to you that I have sent you: when you bring the people out of Egypt, you will all worship God at this mountain." Then Moses asked God, "If I go to the Israelites and say to them: The God of your fathers has sent me to you, and they ask me, 'What is His name?' what should I tell them?" God replied to Moses, "I AM WHO I AM. This is what you are to say to the Israelites: I AM has sent me to you."

— Exodus 3:2-14

Living the way of faith requires you to trust, obey, and rely wholly upon God. The odds will be heaven to one. Dr. Stanley assures us we cannot lose walking in faith. Do you want to achieve and be the best you can be? Or do you want second best? You are blessed because it is up to you to make that decision. Your two choices are your selfish way or trusting, obeying, and relying upon God.

Your holy counsel of God is in print in a language you can understand and trust in every word. God promises in your lifetime you will be faced with a critical decision you must make, and the correct decision is the way of faith. It not only identifies you spiritually but measures your success. Rebellion against God hinders success. Too much focus on position, prestige, and money is embedded in our minds and not focused upon God, therefore, blocking any future success.

Dr. Stanley suggests that you take the first step, and learn to obey, trust, and rely on God. Allow Him to work on the next step. Sometimes the way of faith is the longest, but it is the only way to eternity. You can choose to trust God fully, for He will use anyone who desires to follow Him. Your responsibility is to focus on and follow God's way of faith. Please remember, you are to be the best representative for the Heavenly Father.

God loves you, and this is His wish for you.

Dr. Charles Stanley – Sermon Notes – October 4, 2020 - THE FAITH THAT CONQUERS

Do you find yourself becoming overwhelmed with different battles in your life? Maybe your circumstances seem to be out of control to the point of being threatening and embarrassing. Dr. Stanley explains that the greatest defense you can use during this difficult time — a strong faith in God. It is with faith that we succeed in conquering these challenges. Your faith is based on the foundation of the living God and His word. Many of us know the spectacular story about David facing the Philistine giant Goliath with his sling, a smooth stone, and his faith in the God. Although this was amazing, the real lesson is trusting God when you're faced with a seemingly hopeless situation. Learn how you can stand strong in your battles.

> *The Philistines were standing on one hill, and the Israelites were standing on another hill with a ravine between them. Then a champion named Goliath, from Gath, came out from the Philistine camp. He was nine feet, nine inches tall and wore a bronze helmet and bronze scale armor that weighed 125 pounds. There was bronze armor on his shins, and a bronze sword was slung between his shoulders. His spear shaft was like a weaver's beam, and the iron point of his spear weighed 15 pounds.*
>
> — 1 Samuel 17:3-7

> *David said to Saul, "Don't let anyone be discouraged by him; your servant will go and fight this Philistine!"*

But Saul replied, "You can't go fight this Philistine. You're just a youth, and he's been a warrior since he was young." David answered Saul, "Your servant has been tending his father's sheep. Whenever a lion or a bear came and carried off a lamb from the flock, I went after it, struck it down, and rescued [the lamb] from its mouth. If it reared up against me, I would grab it by its fur, strike it down, and kill it. Your servant has killed lions and bears; this uncircumcised Philistine will be like one of them, for he has defied the armies of the living God." Then David said, "The Lord who rescued me from the paw of the lion and the paw of the bear will rescue me from the hand of this Philistine." Saul said to David, "Go, and may the Lord be with you."

– 1 Samuel 17:32-37

The principles of faith that conquer are:

1. Recall previous victories when facing a battle.
2. Re-exam and re-affirm the proper motive.
3. Faith that conquers reject discouraging words from others. Question your counsel?

Be careful to whom you listen to for people often will say things like, "You do not deserve to be treated this way." God may allow hurtfulness to remain within you because He is building you up and shaping you into His likeness.

We all have certain Goliaths in our lives. You must ask yourself, "What is the purpose to seek this victory?" Will you use your faith and trust in God, or will you go alone?

David put his hand in the bag, took out a stone, slung [it], and hit the Philistine on his forehead. The stone sank into his forehead, and he fell on his face to the ground. David defeated the Philistine with a sling and a stone. Even though David had no sword, he struck down the Philistine and killed him.

— 1 Samuel 17:49-50

We can all be like King David when confronted with battles. Trust in God when you're faced with a seemingly hopeless situation.

God loves you, and this is His wish for you.

Dr. Charles Stanley – Sermon Notes – October 17, 2020 – UNSHAKABLE FAITH

Have you ever faced a financial problem or a physical illness? Dr. Stanley teaches how to stand strong in the face of overwhelming adversity by discussing the life of Daniel. Please read the complete Book of Daniel, which explains how one man's character overcame adversity amongst Babylon, Kings, lions, captivity, and a jealous plot of death.

What does it take to shake your faith? Is it receiving bad news, such as health issues or the loss of a loved one? Could it be a plan that did not go your way? Did it rattle your faith? Dr. Stanley says the key element to unshakable faith is you cannot have it without consistent obedience. You are encouraged to look at the pattern of obedience in your life. Are you living in obedience to God's commands? If not, are you correcting your behavior to be in obedience to God? When He commands you to do something, you do not need to know why. The reason is your loyalty, love, and trust in God. Your lifestyle should be in line with His commands.

Your faith stops growing until you live and understand faith and obedience. People who understand unshakable faith can hear it, see it, and let it go. People of unshakable faith have the wisdom to understand there will be trials, storms, difficulties, brokenness, disappointments, and possibly even death. There is no passage in the Bible that says living by faith is going to be easy, Dr. Stanley teaches.

Keep these words near to your heart — **you cannot have unshakable faith without consistency in obedience**. We all can be like Daniel and learn to stand strong despite overwhelming adversity. When we trust and obey God, He will not fight our battles for us, but he will assist. Dr. Stanley says, "If you love God, you will do what God says, live a life of unshakable faith and consistency in obedience."

God loves you, and this is His wish for you.

83

Dr. Charles Stanley – Sermon Notes – October 25, 2020 - UNSHAKABLE FAITH – Part 2

What does it take to sustain your faith in God? Are you easily rattled when things don't go your way? Do you find yourself asking, "Where is God when I need Him the most? If God loves me, why is He allowing this mess to happen in the first place?"

What does it mean to have unshakable faith? It is not being intimidated and not being rattled by remarks of others. It is being fixed and firm in decision-making. It is steadfastness in faith. Unshakable faith means there is closeness and open communication with God. Unshakable faith is taught by both parents. It is an intimate relationship between you and God. Dr. Stanley reminds us that living in faith does not guarantee things will go smoothly.

The best example of unshakeable faith is in the Book of Daniel, and I encourage you to read Daniel 6:10-18— Daniel in the Lions' Den.

Daniel knew he had an intimate relationship with God as a young child. He desired to know God and to be a companion with Him. Daniel did not have to change a thing, because he walked in faith daily. Daniel developed trust and fellowship with God to sustain his unshakable faith.

Does God seem distant to you? Do you see God as someone whom is up in heaven while you are down here on earth? It does not have to be that way, Dr. Stanley says. Every time you pray, it is in the presence of our Heavenly Father, no matter where you are physically present.

People who understand unshakable faith can hear it, see it, and let it go. People of unshakable faith have the wisdom to understand there will be trials, storms, difficulties, brokenness, and disappointments. Be the best you can by staying focused on God and blocking out all disturbances. A wise person will understand the importance of wanting God in their life.

God loves you, and this is His wish for you.

84

Dr. Charles Stanley – Sermon Notes – November 1, 2020 – THE MISSIONARY CALL

God issues three calls to every single person. First is the call to salvation. The second is the call to sanctification – to bring our conversation, our conduct, and our character under the Lordship of Jesus Christ. The third call is to give ourselves in service to God by serving other people.

"How many of these calls have you answered?" asks Dr. Stanley. A missionary may be a schoolteacher, a carpenter, a preacher, or a group of persons who dare to serve others. Dr. Stanley encourages his listeners to ask God to speak to their hearts, "Lord where do you choose to send me?" A call to missionary work is a divine call, and our responsibility is to say "yes" to God. Please do not bargain with God nor fight against a call from God. Forget about all the "buts." The only responsibility we have is to say, "yes". God will equip us with his plan and his wisdom in our missionary work with our helper, the Holy Spirit. Refreshing to note, wherever we go, God is right there, too. Scripture says, "I promise to never leave nor forsake you." God takes care of those who serve him. God will not send you to serve until you tell Him you are ready. Receiving a call of mission service may take years. If that is the case, God is building faith and encouragement within you to take on one of the biggest challenges of a lifetime. Missionary work is not easy; there will be times of depression, times the communication is poor, and times where you are not seeing any rewards.

Missionary work involves the family. Children have questions, "Mom and Dad, why are you doing this to us?" If God loves us, why is He sending us to another country? In some cases, a man has the desire to serve, but his wife is opposed. However, God has a way of changing her mind. In the family, there may be hate, anger, and hostility. However, there will be times of happiness and joyfulness as missionaries educate and connect with people by the gospel. Dr. Stanley mentions all uncertainties families have; God will fix. Missionary work requires loyalty and devotion. The people we love the most must understand God's call of mission and His ways of serving others. When God calls, He is requiring us to raise our support for others. Every person must do their part. What happens if you fail to meet the needs of others? God knows this will happen, but He also will give us the power and strength to carry out our missionary work. When this happens, we are to look at the cross and ask ourselves, "Does anything ever equal that?" Our Lord Jesus Christ perished on the cross to pay the price for our sins.

Are you going to be ready when God issues three calls to you — salvation, sanctification, and service?

God loves you, and this is His wish for you.

85

**Dr. Charles Stanley – Sermon Notes –
November 8, 2020 – MADE FOR PRAISE**

Praise is not something new. It is not man-made. It is not some theological strain or denominational hand me down. It is a command of the Word of God. In this message, you learn that, as a believer, are to proclaim God's excellence because you are no longer in darkness but have been called into His marvelous light.

God is doing all the talking, and you are His unfinished masterpiece, and you have been chosen. Every single Christian is a member of a royal priesthood. You and I have a kingly heritage. No matter what background we came from, we are related to the King of Kings. Please do not feel you are not important. God has never told you that. These words are from Satan and not God. Remember who is doing the talking. God would never say you do not count. You and I have a royal lineage we become a holy nation.

The Bible says we are people of God's possession. We are more important than any child of any earthly king that has ever lived. We have the lineage of the heavenly King; we are a royal priesthood. One of your responsibilities as a child of God is to worship our Lord. It is to praise Him, that's who you are. You are the priest of God living on this earth. You and I are a lineage of the royal priesthood, the chosen nation, a holy nation. You and I are part of the Body of Jesus Christ, that's who we are. When God looks upon us, He sees us as holy and chosen by Him, that is how God sees us. God has made us his special people for His very own possession. You and I are God's possession. We have been purchased for a price. God loves you and me enough that he gave his only begotten son Jesus Christ who shed his blood on Calvary. Therefore, you and I are the purchased personal possession of almighty God through Jesus Christ, that's who we are. We are His and His alone. God has made us special people for a special purpose. From God's viewpoint, we are his possession, therefore, we are to proclaim the excellencies of Him, who has called us out of the darkness. To praise our Lord Jesus Christ, we are to applaud Him for who He is. We must understand praise and what's involved. Praise is to applaud God for His mighty deeds and mighty acts and we are to celebrate. Make a joyful noise unto the Lord. To lift high His name, it is to love and adore him. Praise is something we are. When you're in love with somebody you cannot keep it quiet. That is the same expression of praise we must have for God.

Please read Psalms 100 — Be Thankful

> *Shout triumphantly to the Lord, all the earth. Serve the Lord with gladness; come before Him with joyful songs. Acknowledge that the Lord is God. He made us, and we are His - His people, the sheep of His pasture. Enter His gates with thanksgiving and His courts with praise. Give thanks to Him and praise His name. For the Lord is good, and His love is eternal; His faithfulness endures through all generations.*
>
> *— Psalms 100:1-5*

There are requirements of praise, and it is to understand who Jesus is. Recognize your sinfulness, confess your sins to Him. Ask Him to save you based not on your righteousness but what He did on Calvary. Ask Him to come into your life and to be to you only what He can be, that's what you call salvation. The new birth, conversion, redemption, justification — all these big names for you, in essence, is God reaching down forgiving your sins, and making you one of his own. Until then, you'll never learn what life's about until you trust the Lord Jesus Christ as your savior. Please remember, it is critical to understand who Jesus is, realize God is doing all the talking, and we are His unfinished masterpiece.

God loves you, and this is His wish for you.

**Dr. Charles Stanley – Sermon Notes – November 15, 2020
- PREPARATION FOR PRAISE**

What is necessary to truly praise and worship God? Can someone just show up at a church and start praising and worshipping God? In this message, Dr. Stanley explains that, oftentimes, people make a lot of preparation to attend church but don't prepare to truly praise the living God. Do not play lip service to God anymore. Learn to worship Him in spirit and truth.

Busy are the families getting ready for church on Sundays. Fixing breakfast, setting clothes out, getting the children ready, and watching the clock on the wall. These are all the tasks we do in preparation to praise God.

The Book of John 4, Jesus and the Samaritan Woman, is an example of understanding the correct way to prepare, praise, and worship with God.

We must understand real praise is the response of truth. Genuine praise is built on the truth. If your praise is not right with God and is not built on the foundation of truth, it will fizzle out. True genuine praise is built on the truth.

Here is a checklist for preparing, praising, and worshipping our Living God:

1. Do you understand preparing and admitting the truth in what you are praising?

2. Do you have the correct spirit? Do you understand the spirit of submission to our Lord Jesus Christ? A rebellious heart cannot praise God.
3. Do you understand what it means to repent of your sin? Never to hold onto secrets or grudges. Sin is a powerful barrier between you and God.
4. What is your relationship with other people like?
5. Are you overcome with anger and negativity just because you did not get your way, or someone hurt you badly?

God desires that you lay aside all bitterness and negativity in your heart, knowing that our Heavenly Father has something far better for you to do with your life. Once you start to prepare and praise our Lord correctly, it changes your perspective on everything you do in life. Dr. Stanley warns to beware of certain hang-ups, such as fear and tradition. Realizing God is of the scriptures, and He does not get hung up on tradition nor fears. Lay aside these emotions and allow God to cleanse your heart and fill it full of thankfulness, love, peace, and joyfulness. Christians are a chosen nation of royal priesthood. You are God's private possession because He loves us, and you love Him. To praise God correctly is to know His attributes, His majestic power, to know why and what He stands for. To praise the Lord, your life must be God-centered. Everything we do must be God-centered. All day long, we must praise God and have a true genuine understanding of His mighty works. Think of God and His genuine love with no competition. Our attention is based upon what's best for God and not what's best for us. Learn to worship Him in spirit and truth.

God loves you, and this is His wish for you.

87

Dr. Charles Stanley – Sermon Notes – November 22, 2020 - THE POWER OF PRAISE IN TIMES OF TROUBLE

When you think of praise, times of happiness and good fortune probably come to mind. What about when seasons of difficulty, hardship, and persecution come, though? Is praise still appropriate then? According to Dr. Stanley, you and I will never understand the real power of praise until we go through tough times.

> *For no matter how many promises God has made, they are "Yes" in Christ. And so through him the "Amen" is spoken by us to the glory of God. Now it is God who makes both us and you stand firm in Christ. He anointed us, set his seal of ownership on us, and put his Spirit in our hearts as a deposit, guaranteeing what is to come. I call God as my witness—and I stake my life on it—that it was in order to spare you that I did not return to Corinth. Not that we lord it over your faith, but we work with you for your joy, because it is by faith you stand firm.*
>
> *– 2 Corinthians 1:20-24*

What is your first reaction when hardship comes your way? Do you start to immediately shut down and feel sorry for yourself? Do you feel as if the hole is too deep? Here are the Twelve Principles of the Power of Praise in Times of Trouble:

1.   Honor God's sovereignty.
2.   Recall all the mighty acts of God.

3. Show thanksgiving. Thank the Lord for hearing your cries. Thank Him for your tears.
4. Enlarge your vision of God, by trusting in our Lord Jesus Christ and understanding what He did on the cross.
5. Magnify the presence of God.
6. Our faith in God increases and blessings start to flow.
7. Realize praise is the prerequisite to knowing the will of God.
8. Allow God to show you what to do every time.
9. Praise will exalt the name above all names.
10. Praise releases the power of God, allowing Him to demonstrate His supernatural power just in time.
11. Praise unites the people of God.
12. Praise fills the heart with the joy of our Lord Jesus Christ.

Praise paves the way for your independence, as you seek a fresh start and focus on God as your director. It is only through God that we feel the safest in times of trouble. Please keep in mind, you and I will never fully understand the real power of praise until we go through tough times. It is through the power of praise in times of trouble that you see God's supernatural power being released upon you.

God loves you, and this is His wish for you.

88

Dr. Charles Stanley – Sermon Notes – November 28, 2020 – A GLIMPSE OF HEAVENLY PRAISE

One of the primary reasons that people spend so little time praising the Lord is because of a inadequate understanding of who He is. In this message, Dr. Stanley explains that when you begin to understand how Holy, majestic, and mighty God is, you begin to understand how to praise and worship Him.

If you find it difficult to praise and pray, Dr. Stanley adds, just get down on your knees and cry out, "Holy, holy, holy Lord God, the Almighty, who was, who is, and who is to come."

Now I want you to know, brothers, that the gospel preached by me is not based on a human point of view. For I did not receive it from a human source, and I was not taught it, but it came by a revelation from Jesus Christ. For you have heard about my former way of life in Judaism: I persecuted God's church to an extreme degree and tried to destroy it; and I advanced in Judaism beyond many contemporaries among my people, because I was extremely zealous for the traditions of my ancestors. But when God, who from my mother's womb set me apart and called me by His grace, was pleased to reveal His Son in me, so that I could preach Him among the Gentiles, I did not immediately consult with anyone. I did not go up to Jerusalem to those who had become apostles before me; instead, I went to Arabia and came back to Damascus.

— Galatians 1:11-17

Did you know that once you become a Christian there is this incredible certain transformation that takes place, and you cannot keep it quiet? Family and friends are interested in your changed personality and want to know more about you. It enables you to introduce God as your very best friend. As born-again Christians, we have learned the correct and honorable way to praise and understand God, but only if we listen to the Holy Spirit's guidance and stay in the word. Start today to think of God as your majestic, powerful, kind, loving savior. God is seen as a radiant figure, a love for mankind. It is only through praise and worship you start to see who God is.

The Book of Revelation is preparing us for God's return, and you can learn more reading Revelation 1:1-8 — Prologue; Revelation 4:1-11 — The Throne Room of Heaven; and Revelation 5:1-6 — The Lamb Takes the Scroll.

The next time you get a glimpse of heavenly praise, get down on your knees and pray Holy, holy, holy Lord God Almighty, who was, who is, and who is to come.

God loves you, and this is His wish for you.

89

Dr. Charles Stanley – Sermon Notes – December 5, 2020 - THE RISK OF OBEYING GOD

When God calls people to serve Him, He may assign them God-sized tasks that are beyond their abilities. He does so because He wants to show His power through them. Are you afraid to step out in faith because of the possible hazards ahead of you? Find the courage because you need to follow God's call. When it comes to God's calling, do not miss the load of blessings.

One of the main reasons you may disregard God's calling is a fear of failure. You are not sure what God wants you to do, and you let the fear of failure stand in the way. You become uncertain about your trust and faith in God. Maybe there is a fear of losing control and you must surrender.

When God calls you to do something, it is because He loves you and it is through love that God demonstrates His power.

> *When He had finished speaking, He said to Simon, "Put out into deep water and let down your nets for a catch." "Master," Simon replied, "we've worked hard all night long and caught nothing! But at Your word, I'll let down the nets." When they did this, they caught a great number of fish, and their nets began to tear. So, they signaled to their partners in the other boat to come and help them; they came and filled both boats so full that they began to sink. When Simon Peter saw this, he fell at Jesus' knees and said, "Go away from me, because I'm a sinful man, Lord!" For he and all those with him*

*were amazed at the catch of fish they took, and so were
James and John, Zebedee's sons, who were Simon's
partners. "Don't be afraid," Jesus told Simon. "From
now on you will be catching people!" Then they brought
the boats to land, left everything, and followed Him.*

— Luke 5:4-11

The message here is that when you obey God's calling, not only
is God blessing you but others as well. When you obey God, you
start to realize what He is all about, and His supernatural power.
Sometimes God will instruct you to do the opposite of what
everyone around you is doing, which may seem very unnatural.
If you do what God tells you to do, you will never come up with
an empty net. When God tells you to do something, it's because
He loves you.

Ask yourself this question, how many blessings have you missed
because you have not obeyed God's calling? Dr. Stanley says we
are all guilty of this. When God requests something from you,
do you put up a private sign to whatever God is asking? God
does not operate with private signs. God desires that you obey
and receive His abundant blessings. Allow God to hold up His
blessings for you. God may request a simple call first. Dr. Stanley
also tells younger people, "God will test you first, to see if you
have obeyed His simple calls. God is examining your heart he
wants you to clean it up. He wants you to demonstrate how you
handle the simple call first."

There are people around you watching your life, and it is your
responsibility to be the best representative of our Lord Jesus
Christ. They may not tell you, but after watching your obedience
and changing lives, that is what they want to.

Allow God to work in your life and ask Him, "Lord what do you want me to do?" God may give you a simple call or a big call. It is a tragedy to miss God's load of blessings.

God loves you, and this is His wish for you.

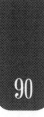

90

Dr. Charles Stanley – Sermon Notes – December 20, 2020 – OUR GREAT HIGH PRIEST

Definition of Redemption – to deliver from sin; to restore; to make amends or atone for

Definition of Sanctification – holiness, holy

Definition of Sacred – consecrated to a god or God, holy, having to do with religion

Definition of Sympathized – to share the feelings or ideas of others; to feel or express sympathy

Definition of Venerate – to worship; to look upon with feelings of deep respect

Why is it that some people perceive the Christian life as an exciting journey and others see it as a burdensome, unfulfilling existence? Do not be fooled and think your strength and goodness is the only way in which you need to live your life, Dr. Stanley explains. It is a privilege to have Christ as your mediator and advocate, Dr. Stanley adds and His role as your High Priest is meant to set you free to enjoy intimate and trustful relations with God.

In the Bible, there are differing opinions of who is the great High Priest, but clarification is in the scriptures of Mathew, John, and Hebrews.

> *You are the light of the world. A city situated on a hill cannot be hidden. No one lights a lamp and puts it*

under a basket, but rather on a lampstand, and it gives light for all who are in the house. In the same way, let your light shine before men, so that they may see your good works and give glory to your Father in heaven.

— Mathew 5:14-16

Others said, "This is the Messiah!" But some said, "Surely the Messiah doesn't come from Galilee, does He? Doesn't the Scripture say that the Messiah comes from David's offspring and from the town of Bethlehem, where David once lived?" So a division occurred among the crowd because of Him. Some of them wanted to seize Him, but no one laid hands on Him. Then the temple police came to the chief priests and Pharisees, who asked them, "Why haven't you brought Him?" The police answered, "No man ever spoke like this!"

— John 7: 41-46

For every high priest taken from men is appointed in service to God for the people, to offer both gifts and sacrifices for sins. He is able to deal gently with those who are ignorant and are going astray, since he himself is also subject to weakness. Because of this, he must make a sin offering for himself as well as for the people.

— Hebrews 5:1-3

Our great High Priest Jesus Christ is more than just a miracle baby in a manger. He has the power of redemption and sanctification. He amends for all wrongdoing. Our Lord Jesus Christ desires to cleanse and purify your heart. It is a rebirth with a clean slate. Instantly, you become a Child of God. Christ is sympathetic to your feelings, pain, and agony. Christ knows exactly what you are going through and promises never to leave you in times of trouble.

The first thing in the morning until bedtime, He knows exactly what you are experiencing. Do you feel tired of your old ways and desire to want more of God into your life? First, you must ask forgiveness and be willing to deal with your sinful ways. Openly acknowledge Jesus Christ as your savior. Acknowledge that Jesus Christ died for all our sins so that we may spend eternal life with our Heavenly Father. Jesus makes it possible to immediately start building a foundation and relationship with Him once you are willing to surrender.

Do you have a better deal than this? Acknowledge our great High Priest is our Lord Jesus Christ. Live in harmony with our Heavenly Father. Trust and obey instead of allowing darkness and guilt to dominate your life. Free yourself from wrongdoing and other sins. God tells us he is waiting and anticipating your arrival. His role as our High Priest is meant to set us free, so we can enjoy an intimate and fruitful relationship with God.

God loves you, and this is His wish for you.

91

Dr. Charles Stanley – Sermon Notes – December 25, 2020 – THE BIRTH OF JESUS

In those days a decree went out from Caesar Augustus 14; also known as Octavian, he established the peaceful era known as the Pax Romana; Caesar was a title of Roman emperors. that the whole empire should be registered. This first registration took place while Quirinius was governing Syria. So, everyone went to be registered, each to his own town. And Joseph also went up from the town of Nazareth in Galilee to Judea, to the city of David, which is called Bethlehem, because he was of the house and family line of David, to be registered along with Mary, who was engaged to him and was pregnant. While they were there, the time came for her to give birth. Then she gave birth to her firstborn Son, and she wrapped Him snugly in cloth and laid Him in a feeding trough-because there was no room for them at the inn.

– Luke 2:1-7

In the same region, shepherds were staying out in the fields and keeping watch at night over their flock. Then an angel of the Lord stood before them, and the glory of the Lord shone around them, and they were terrified. But the angel said to them, "Don't be afraid, for look, I proclaim to you good news of great joy that will be for all the people: today a Savior, who is Messiah the Lord, was born for you in the city of David. This will be the sign for you: you will find a baby wrapped snugly in cloth and lying in a feeding trough."

– Luke 2: 8-12

Why did God send the 3 Kings Men? They brought silver and gold, but they were looking for a bigger payout!

Why did God send the Shepherds? They were not men of wealth and were lower-class citizens!

Why did God send Angels? They were God's special messengers and people believed in them. An angel of the Lord stood before them, and the glory of the Lord shone around them, and they were terrified. But the angel said to them, "Don't be afraid, for look, I proclaim to you good news of great joy that will be for all the people. Today a Savior was born for you, who is the Messiah."

God loves you, and this is His wish for you.

92

Dr. Charles Stanley – Sermon Notes -January 2, 2021 - THE TEN COMMANDMENTS and WHERE TO TURN WHEN THE EVIL IN THE WORLD SEEMS OVERWHELMING

Allow the new year to bring a clean slate into your life. Start the new year with a refresher of The Ten Commandments:

Then God spoke all these words:
I am the Lord your God, who brought you out of the land of Egypt, out of the place of slavery.
Do not have other gods besides Me.
Do not make an idol for yourself, whether in the shape of anything in the heavens above or on the earth below or in the waters under the earth.You must not bow down to them or worship them; for I, the Lord your God, am a jealous God, punishing the children for the fathers' sin, to the third and fourth [generations] of those who hate Me, but showing faithful love to a thousand [generations] of those who love Me and keep My commands.
Do not misuse the name of the Lord your God, because the Lord will punish anyone who misuses His name.
Remember to dedicate the Sabbath day: You are to labor six days and do all your work, but the seventh day is a Sabbath to the Lord your God. You must not do any work-you, your son or daughter, your male or female slave, your livestock, or the foreigner who is within your gates. For the Lord made the heavens and the earth, the sea, and everything in them in six days; then He

rested on the seventh day. Therefore, the Lord blessed the Sabbath day and declared it holy.

Honor your father and your mother so that you may have a long life in the land that the Lord your God is giving you.

Do not murder.

Do not commit adultery.

Do not steal.

Do not give false testimony against your neighbor.

Do not covet your neighbor's house. Do not covet your neighbor's wife, his male or female slave, his ox or donkey, or anything that belongs to your neighbor.

— Exodus 20:1-17

Also take a moment to understand where to turn when evil in the world seems overwhelming:

For I consider that the sufferings of this present time are not worth comparing with the glory that is going to be revealed to us. For the creation eagerly wait with anticipation of God's sons to be revealed.

— Romans 8:18-19

God loves you, and this is His wish for you.

93

Dr. Charles Stanley – Sermon Notes – January 9, 2021 – GOD IS

In this sermon, Dr. Stanley asks, "How can we conclude there is a God?" The answer will equip you in times of doubt and the questioning by others. Human reason, divine revelation, and personal experience all work together to affirm God's existence. It all begins in the books of Genesis and ends in Revelation.

In the beginning, God created the heavens and the earth.
– Genesis 1:1

The revelation of Jesus Christ that God gave Him to show His slaves what must quickly take place. He sent it and signified it through His angel to His slave John, who testified to God's word and to the testimony about Jesus Christ, in all he saw. Blessed is the one who reads and blessed are those who hear the words of this prophecy and keep what is written in it, because the time is near! John: To the seven churches in the province of Asia. Grace and peace to you from the One who is, who was, and who is coming; from the seven spirits before His throne; and from Jesus Christ, the faithful witness, the firstborn from the dead and the ruler of the kings of the earth. To Him who loves us and has set us free from our sins by His blood, and made us a kingdom, priests to His God and Father-to Him be the glory and dominion forever and ever. Amen. Look! He is coming with the clouds, and every eye will see Him, including those who pierced

Him. And all the families of the earth will mourn over
Him. This is certain. Amen.

— Revelation 1:1-7

How do we explain our solar system and its nine planets in their perfect order? How do we explain the perfect timing of the seasons? How did all of this happen? It is very clear, year after year, how a scientist can perfectly justify these superpowers. There is no one, other than our Heavenly Father, who could have created them, therefore, "God Is." God has given you the Bible for all your questions and answers to mankind. Your job is to use it as your guide in your everyday life. When you surrender to God and His divine salvation, you must give up all your sins and live for Him. It is a transformation that takes place. You'll find yourself ripping into the Bible. You'll find yourself seeking more accountability, more holiness, more justice, and more judgment. You'll not just whisper, "Yes" to God, but you'll be shouting at the top of your lungs, "Hallelujah!" God will live in your heart for everlasting eternity.

For I am not ashamed of the gospel, because it is God's
power for salvation to everyone who believes, first to the
Jew, and also to the Greek. For in it God's righteousness
is revealed from faith to faith, just as it is written: The
righteous will live by faith.

— Romans 1:16-17

It is helpful and important when speaking to a non-believer, that you ask the questions first — is God real? How can we conclude there is a God? By our human reason, by our divine revelation, and by our personal experience all working to glorify and affirm, "God Is."

"Your heart must not be troubled. Believe in God; believe also in Me. In My Father's house are many dwelling places; a traveler's resting place. The Gk word is related to the verb meno, meaning remain or stay which occurs 40 times in John; if not, I would have told you. I am going away to prepare a place for you. If I go away and prepare a place for you, I will come back and receive you to Myself, so that where I am you may be also. You know the way where I am going."

"Lord," Thomas said, "we don't know where You're going. How can we know the way?" Jesus told him, "I am the way, the truth, and the life. No one comes to the Father except through Me. If you know Me, you will also know My Father. From now on you do know Him and have seen Him."

— John 14:1-7

Can you think of a better plan than this? Dr. Stanley asks.

God loves you, and this is His wish for you.

94

**Dr. Charles Stanley – Sermon Notes –
January 16, 2021 – GOD IS REAL?**

Who is Jesus? How can you conclude there is a God? Did you know God does not mess up? God's promises are true. God desires for you to have eternal life with Him in heaven, where there is no evil, no sickness, and no hate. How do you know and understand His reasons? The scriptures will answer all your questions:

> *I am the true vine, and My Father is the vineyard keeper. Every branch in Me that does not produce fruit He removes, and He prunes every branch that produces fruit so that it will produce more fruit. You are already clean because of the word I have spoken to you. Remain in Me, and I in you. Just as a branch is unable to produce fruit by itself unless it remains on the vine, so neither can you unless you remain in Me. I am the vine; you are the branches. The one who remains in Me and I in him produces much fruit, because you can do nothing without Me.*
>
> *– John 15:1-5*

> *I am the good shepherd. The good shepherd lays down his life for the sheep.*
>
> *– John 10:11*

> *So He got into a boat, crossed over, and came to His own town. Just then some men brought to Him a paralytic lying on a stretcher. Seeing their faith, Jesus told the paralytic, "Have courage, son, your sins are forgiven."*

At this, some of the scribes said among themselves, "He's blaspheming!" But perceiving their thoughts, Jesus said, "Why are you thinking evil things in your hearts? For which is easier: to say, 'Your sins are forgiven,' or to say, 'Get up and walk'? But so you may know that the Son of Man has authority on earth to forgive sins" Then He told the paralytic, "Get up, pick up your stretcher, and go home." And he got up and went home. When the crowds saw this, they were awestruck and gave glory to God who had given such authority to men.

— Matthew 9:1-8

Jesus said to her, "I am the resurrection and the life. The one who believes in Me, even if he dies, will live. Everyone who lives and believes in Me will never die-ever. Do you believe this?

— John 11:25-26

Jesus told him, "I am the way, the truth, and the life. No one comes to the Father except through Me. If you know Me, you will also know My Father. From now on you do know Him and have seen Him."

— John 14:6-7

Blessed be the God and Father of our Lord Jesus Christ. According to His great mercy, He has given us a new birth into a living hope through the resurrection of Jesus Christ from the dead, and into an inheritance that is imperishable, uncorrupted, unfading, kept in heaven for you.

— 1 Peter 1:3-4

They came to Jesus and saw the man who had been demon-possessed by the legion, sitting there, dressed and in his right mind; and they were afraid. The eyewitnesses described to them what had happened to the demon-possessed man and [told] about the pigs. Then they began to beg Him to leave their region. As He was getting into the boat, the man who had been demon-possessed kept begging Him to be with Him. But He would not let him; instead, He told him, "Go back home to your own people, and report to them how much the Lord has done for you and how He has had mercy on you."

— Mark 5:15-19

"I am the bread of life," Jesus told them. "No one who comes to Me will ever be hungry, and no one who believes in Me will ever be thirsty again. But as I told you, you've seen Me, and yet you do not believe. Everyone the Father gives Me will come to Me, and the one who comes to Me I will never cast out. For I have come down from heaven, not to do My will, but the will of Him who sent Me. This is the will of Him who sent Me: that I should lose none of those He has given Me but should raise them up on the last day.

— John 6:35-39

Then Jesus spoke to them again: "I am the light of the world. Anyone who follows Me will never walk in the darkness but will have the light of life."

— John 8:12

I am the door. If anyone enters by Me, he will be saved and will come in and go out and find pasture. A thief comes only to steal and to kill and to destroy. I have come that they may have life and have it in abundance.

— John 10:9-10

Is God real? How can we conclude there is a God? By human reason, by divine revelation, and by personal experiences all working to glorify and affirm, "GOD IS."

It all begins in the book of Genesis and ends in Revelation.

> *Look! He is coming with the clouds, and every eye will see Him, including those who pierced Him. And all the families of the earth will mourn over Him. This is certain. Amen.*
>
> – Revelation 1:7

God does not mess up.

God loves you, and this is His wish for you.

95

Dr. Charles Stanley – Sermon Notes – January 23, 2021, HIS INCOMPARABLE NAME

In this message, Dr. Stanley leads us on a study of the names of God and the attributes of Him that each reveal. There is always more to understand about the One to whom we confess, pray, and offer worship. Learn how each one of God's names is a different expression of His might and faithfulness, inviting us to honor, praise, and "a closer walk with Thee."

What's in a name? Quite a lot, especially when you're talking about God. If you go through the scripture, you find something very comforting. That is, for every emergency that man can find, there is a name about God that meets that emergency. Not just a haphazard name that man has given to Him. You will learn what God wants us to know about His names. Ask God to speak to your heart, and you'll receive a whole new appreciation for His names. There are two primary names — Elohim and Jehovah.

Genesis 1, The Creation, explains the name of Elohim. In the beginning, God created the heavens and the earth. Elohim means strength, power, might, and absolute faithfulness. You can learn more by reading Genesis.

Isaiah 40, talks of the name Jehovah, which means eternal. Being everlasting is the very essence of God. He is self-existing, and the highest of all names.

> *Who will you compare God with? What likeness will you compare Him to? To an idol? [something that]*

a smelter casts, and a metalworker plates with gold and makes silver welds [for it]? To one who shapes a pedestal, choosing wood that does not rot? He looks for a skilled craftsman to set up an idol that will not fall over. Do you not know? Have you not heard? Has it not been declared to you from the beginning? Have you not considered the foundations of the earth? God is enthroned above the circle of the earth; its inhabitants are like grasshoppers. He stretches out the heavens like thin cloth and spreads them out like a tent to live in. He reduces princes to nothing and makes the judges of the earth to be irrational. They are barely planted, barely sown, their stem hardly takes root in the ground when He blows on them and they wither, and a whirlwind carries them away like stubble. "Who will you compare Me to, or who is My equal?" asks the Holy One.

— Isaiah 40:18-25

God is not interested in a man being a leader. He desires for man to be a servant. You may be on the highest pedestal of a leader and, by the request of God, be lowered to dust.

Commander of the Lord's Army. When Joshua was near Jericho, he looked up and saw a man standing in front of him with a drawn sword in his hand. Joshua approached him and asked, "Are you for us or our enemies?" "Neither;" he replied, "I have now come as a commander of the Lord's army." Then Joshua bowed with his face to the ground in worship and asked him, "What does my lord want to say to his servant?" The commander of the Lord's army said to Joshua, "Remove the sandals from your feet, for the place where are standing is holy." And Joshua did that.

— Joshua 5:13-15

Joshua 5:13, There was a Hebrew Law that said, "When a man is required by God to do something he feels incapable of doing, he was asked to take off his shoes which was an act of humility, I'm not worthy." What God wants is a servant spirit. Dr. Stanley asked, "I wonder how many times you and I have done the same thing?" God may say, "You're running your show." God knows we cannot do this task on our strength. God wants us to be strong vigilant servants. When God wants something supernature done what does he do? He takes his leaders to the dust until their willing to say, "Oh God you have total control and authority, it is you who I trust and obey." That is the difference between a leader and a so-called leader.

God desires for us to live correctly and to trust and serve Him. God wants to bring awareness of the holiness of Him. You see, if you and I understand who He is, it will do something for our prayers, it will do something for the ones we love, and it will do something for the calling of His name.

Ask God to speak to your heart and provide a whole new appreciation for His name.

God loves you, and this is His wish for you.

96

Dr. Charles Stanley Sermon Notes - January 31, 2021 - THE CREATION

Definition of Believe – to take as true, real; to trust a statement or a promise of (a person); to suppose or think; to have trust, faith, or confidence; believer

Definition of Real – existing as or in fact; actual; true, authentic; genuine

> *In the beginning, God created the heavens and the earth. Now the earth was formless and empty, darkness covered the surface of the watery depths, and the Spirit of God was hovering over the surface of the waters. Then God said, "Let there be light," and there was light. God saw that the light was good, and God separated the light from the darkness. God called the light "day", and the darkness he called "night". There was an evening, and there was a morning: one day.*

> *Then God said, "Let there be an expanse between the waters, separating water from water". So God made the expanse and separated the water under the expanse from the water above the expanse. And it was so. God called the expanse "sky". The evening came and then morning: the second day.*

> *Then God said, "Let the water under the sky be gathered into one place, and let the dry land appear." And it was so. God called the dry land "earth", and the gathering*

of the water he called "seas." And God saw that it was good. Then God said, "Let the earth produce vegetables: seed-bearing in it according to their kinds." And it was so. The earth produced vegetation; seed-bearing plants according to their kinds and trees bearing fruit with seed in it according to their kinds. And God saw that it was good. Evening came and then morning; the third day

Then God said, "Let there be lights in the expanse of the sky to separate the day from the night. They will serve as signs of seasons and for days and years. They will be lights in the expanse of the sky to provide light on the earth." And it was so. God made the two great lights – the greater light to rule over the day and the lesser light to rule over the night – as well as the stars. God placed them in the expanse of the sky to provide light on the earth, to rule the day and the night, and to separate light from the darkness. And God saw that it was good. The evening came and then morning: the fourth day.

Then God said, "Let the water swarm with living creatures and let birds fly above the earth across the expanse of the sky." So, God created the large sea creatures and every living creature that moves and swarms in the water, according to their kinds. He also created every winged creature according to its kind. And God saw that it was good. God blessed them, "Be fruitful, multiple, and fill the waters of the seas, and let the birds multiply on the earth." Evening came and then morning: the fifth day

Then God said, "Let the earth produce living creatures according to their kinds: livestock, creatures that crawl, *and the wildlife of the earth according to their kinds." And it was so. So, God made the wildlife of the earth according to their kinds, the livestock according to their kinds, and all the creatures that crawl on the ground according to their kinds. And God saw that it was good. Then God said, "Let us make man in our image, according to our likeness. They will rule the fish of the sea, the birds of the sky, the livestock, the whole earth, and the creatures that crawl on the earth." So, God created man in his image; he created him in the image of God; he created them male and female. God blessed them, and God said to them, "Be fruitful, multiply, fill the earth, and subdue it. Rule the fish of the sea, the birds of the sky, and every creature that crawls on the earth." God also said, "Look, I have given you every seed-bearing plant on the surface of the entire earth and every tree whose fruit contains seed. This will be food for you, for all the wildlife of the earth, for every bird of the sky, and for every creature that crawls on the earth- everything having the breath of life in it — I have given every green plant for food." And it was so. God saw all that he had made, and it was very good indeed. Evening came and then morning: the sixth day.*

— Genesis 1:1-31

So, the heavens and the earth and everything in them were completed. On the seventh day, God had completed the work that he had done, and he rested on the seventh day from all the work that he had done. God blessed the seventh day and declared it holy, for on it he rested from all his work of creation: the seventh day.

— Genesis 2:1-3

God loves you, and this is His wish for you.

97

Dr. Charles Stanley - Sermon Notes – February 7, 2021 – GOD THE FATHER

In this message, Dr. Stanley addresses how you become a child of God and how you can relate to Him as Father. As believers, we have been accepted by the beloved and adopted into His kingdom. Learning to walk in the assurance of your identity is a daily challenge. But, fully yielding your life to Him allows you to experience, perhaps for the first time, the goodness of the perfect heavenly Father.

Tell me what you think about God. What is his character like? Do you respond, "He is our Creator. God is love, God is justice."? The last characteristic most people would say is, "He is my Father." You must know the Son of God before you know who God is. John 14 is helpful for understanding what Jesus says.

> *"Your heart must not be troubled. Believe in God; believe also in Me. In My Father's house are many dwelling places; a traveler's resting place. The Gk word is related to the verb meno, meaning remain or stay, which occurs 40 times in John. if not, I would have told you. I am going away to prepare a place for you. If I go away and prepare a place for you, I will come back and receive you to Myself, so that where I am you may be also. You know the way where I am going."*

> *"Lord," Thomas said, "we don't know where You're going. How can we know the way?"*

Jesus told him, "I am the way, the truth, and the life. No one comes to the Father except through Me. If you know Me, you will also know My Father. From now on you do know Him and have seen Him."

— John 14:1-7

Our heavenly Father is loving, He is generous and kind. He is an intimate God who desires to be the Father of all mankind. God wants to get down to our level. God desires to bring us up to his level.

Dr. Stanley says there is one correct statement when speaking of the universal God. Do you believe in the universal God? The Bible says, "God is everybody's God, the Father of all mankind. He is not one of judgment." Please read the following scriptures regarding the one God, the creator, and the Fatherhood of God. The difference is significant.

Don't all of us have one Father? Didn't one God create us? Why then do we act treacherously against one another, profaning the covenant of our Fathers?

— Malachi 2:10

Then Paul stood in the middle of the Areopagus and said: "Men of Athens! I see that you are extremely religious in every respect. For as I was passing through and observing the objects of your worship, I even found an altar on which was inscribed: TO AN UNKNOWN GOD Therefore, what you worship in ignorance, this I proclaim to you. The God who made the world and everything in it-He is Lord of heaven and earth and does not live in shrines made by hands.

— Acts 17:22-24

God is the Father to all mankind, but only if people believe in his son, Jesus Christ. Jesus came to earth for many reasons, but the primary one was to die for us. It is only through Jesus Christ you may call God your Father. Why? Because you have been saved and have experienced a personal relationship with him. Immediately, you are adopted into God's family and now called a child of God. There is no other way you can call God your Father. It is biblically written you must be born again. There is no such thing as the universal Father of God. God is only the Father of the Creator and that's it.

Make this year the one to become a child of God. God is patiently waiting for you to make the most important decision of your life. God desires for you to experience eternity in Heaven. Is there anything more important than believing in our Lord Jesus Christ and his plan for your life? Talk to God today, tell him you surrender, tell him you repent for all your sins, tell him you believe in Jesus Christ as your savior, tell God you want to serve him and walk in his grace, to be the best representative you can be. Express your wisdom and thankfulness by yielding your life over to God. Every day, honor and be proud to call God, "My Father."

God loves you, and this is His wish for you.

98

**Dr. Charles Stanley – Sermon Notes –
February 13, 2021 – LIKE A ROCK**

As a believer, your citizenship is in heaven. Our Savior, the Lord Jesus Christ, by the power that enables Him to subject all things to Himself, will transform your earthly body to a glorious one.

Simple disputes are not bad, and God tells us to rejoice in all circumstances. If things get out of hand, you just need to recenter and follow the disciplines of poise, prayer, and presence. True Christians have a better way of understanding how this works. By this method, we unite and stand strong. You must remember never to forget your position, nor what Jesus has done for you. In all circumstances, look towards what Jesus has done for you. All other matters instantly become secondary. We are disciples of our Lord Jesus Christ. Think about this picture. God opens the door, and we are all seated around His table. God walks in with his arms fully extended out and says, "I've got this taken care of and you do not need to worry about a thing." God wants us to always trust in Him. Look to God and only lean into God.

Believe in God when he says there is a limit to sadness. In time, God lessens your sadness. When God allows sadness, remember He is building you up. God will test your faith. If your faith is out of line, God will try something else. Our job is to trust, seek God's peace and never stop. Our Lord has made a blueprint for every one of us, and the sadness He allows is limited. God desires you to dwell in eternal things, like heaven or your future.

Do you worry about worrying? Stop and find peace in the principles of poise, prayer, and presence. Let your reason be known to everyone.

"Be bold, be brave, be forthright, and the bold, the brave, and the forthright will gather around you." John Lewis

> *So then, in this way, my dearly loved brothers, my joy*
> *and crown, stand firm in the Lord, dear friends.*
> — Philippians 4:1

We can all find peace in the principles of poise, prayer, and presence.

God loves you, and this is His wish for you.

99

Dr. Charles Stanley – Sermon Notes –
February 21, 2021 – JESUS THE SAVIOR

God's ultimate purpose in sending Jesus Christ into the world was to save us from sin. But what precisely did He save? Our bodies, souls, spirits, minds, wills, or emotions? Sin has a profound impact on every part of your being. Each sin underscores your desperate need for a Savior.

The people during this period of history were looking for a deliverer or a Messiah. The primary reason for God to send Jesus Christ into the world was to break the power of Romans, so the Jewish people may be free as a nation. God's ultimate purpose in sending Jesus into the world was to deal with the sin mankind had created.

Please read Matthew 1 – The Genealogy of Jesus Christ to understand more about how Jesus came into the world.

> *...and Jacob fathered Joseph the husband of Mary, who gave birth to Jesus who is called the Messiah. So, all the generations from Abraham to David were 14 generations; and from David until the exile to Babylon, 14 generations; and from the exile to Babylon until the Messiah, 14 generations. The birth of Jesus Christ came about this way: After His mother Mary had been engaged to Joseph, it was discovered before they came together that she was pregnant by the Holy Spirit. So, her husband Joseph, being a righteous man, and not wanting to disgrace her publicly, decided to divorce her*

secretly. But after he had considered these things, an angel of the Lord suddenly appeared to him in a dream, saying, "Joseph, son of David, don't be afraid to take Mary as your wife, because what has been conceived in her is by the Holy Spirit. She will give birth to a son, and you are to name Him Jesus, because He will save His people from their sins." Now all this took place to fulfill what was spoken by the Lord through the prophet: See, the virgin will become pregnant and give birth to a son, and they will name Him Immanuel, which is translated "God is with us."

— Matthew 1:16-23

Every man and woman have experienced sin in their life. God knows you are not capable of dealing with sin on your own. Sin was the problem that brought Jesus into the world. What is it that Jesus came to save? He came to save your spirit, soul, and body.

Now may the God of peace Himself sanctify you completely. And may your spirit, soul, and body be kept sound and blameless for the coming of our Lord Jesus Christ. He who calls you is faithful, who also will do it.

— 1 Thessalonians 5:23-24

This is a wonderful description of how man is made-up. The soul of a man is his mind...the real man. Sin always attempts to make prisoners out of you. Sin is stronger than you. God desires to save you from sin and the consequences of sin, including death. The law of sin and death is going on in the universe all the time, and Jesus Christ came to break its power. God deals with sin in your life, so you are victorious against it. When sin gets into your life, there is pressure, and you are encouraged to wrap up sin with ten tons of rock and sink it into the ocean. Each time you sin, you are breaking the heart of God. He has a bigger and better plan for you and me. He desires to eliminate all sin, to set us free from sin, so we may focus on what matters the most…spending eternal life with Him in heaven.

God loves you, and this is His wish for you.

Dr. Charles Stanley – Sermon Notes – February 28, 2021 – THE THIRD PERSON

In this sermon, Dr. Stanley discussed the Holy Spirit Prayer — *Be with me. Be in me. Be with me. Be in me.*

Who is the Holy Spirit? It is our Lord Jesus Christ.

The Holy Spirit is NOT WEIRD.

The Holy Spirit is a person.

The Holy Spirit is the resident that lives within you.

The Holy Spirit is your friend.

The Holy Spirit will argue with you.

The Holy Spirit sets you free.

The Holy Spirit is your helper.

The Holy Spirit is there through eternity.

How do you know the Holy Spirit is speaking to you? Does it point to Jesus Christ? The Holy Spirit is comprised of two orders, Dr. Stanley explains, which are first-order desires and second-order desires.

First-order desires are the thoughts and behavior of an animal, a burning inside, a killing instinct, craving, a severe lack of control.

Second-order desires are better than the flesh of man, something that is sensational, healthier, a greater willpower. Daily, you are in a battle between these two desires. However, there is hope. You have been blessed with a choice of living a spiritual life. This blessed spirit is called the Holy Spirit. Why is it so important to long for and live a second-order desire? Because there are times in your life being a Christian is not always easy.

> *Remind them to be submissive to rulers and authorities, to obey, to be ready for every good work, to slander no one, to avoid fighting, and to be kind, always showing gentleness to all people. For we too were once foolish, disobedient, deceived, captives of various passions and pleasures, living in malice and envy, hateful, detesting one another. But when the goodness and love for man appeared from God our Savior, He saved us- not by works of righteousness that we had done, but according to His mercy, through the washing of regeneration and renewal by the Holy Spirit.*
>
> *– Titus 3:1-5*

> *Therefore, brothers, by the mercies of God, I urge you to present your bodies as a living sacrifice, holy and pleasing to God; this is your spiritual worship. Do not be conformed to this age, but be transformed by the renewing of your mind, so that you may discern what is the good, pleasing, and perfect will of God.*
>
> *– Romans 12:1-2*

The Holy Spirit is your helper. He will lead and guide you into this transformation and renewal process. Your job is to believe, trust and listen. It is important to discipline yourself to a true and proper way of worship. Allow the Holy Spirit to cleanse, renew and transform your body.

Our third person, The Holy Spirit has the power of turning a wrong into a right. Understanding the ways of Jesus is understanding freedom, forgiveness, peace, love, and eternal life. Please do not miss out on this extraordinary opportunity.

> *Now the Lord is the Spirit; and where the Spirit of the Lord is, there is freedom. We all, with unveiled faces, are reflecting the glory of the Lord and are being transformed into the same image from glory to glory; this is from the Lord who is the Spirit.*
>
> — 2 Corinthians 3:17-18

Living a life without God and relying on your willpower is a dangerous thing. Sooner or later your willpower runs out. Your part is a partnership with the Holy Spirit. You must understand that the Holy Spirit does not do all the work nor all the heavy lifting. You must help yourself as well. This is from the Lord who is the Spirit.

Today, allow the Holy Spirit through His power to turn a wrong into a right. That's how much our Heavenly Father loves you and me, knowing He is willing and capable of turning a wrong into a right.

God loves you, and this is His wish for you.

Dr. Charles Stanley – Sermon Notes – March 7, 2021 – THE CHARACTER OF GOD

Definition of Character — a distinctive trait, quality, etc.; characteristic kind or sort behavior typical of a person or group; moral strength reputation, status; position

Definition of Sovereign — super, above all others; chief, supreme, supreme in power, rank, independent of all others; a monarch or ruler

Dr. Stanley encourages us to read the following books in the Bible to clarify and understand who God is and what God's character is like. Who is God? He is our way maker, our miracle worker, and a promise keeper.

God created the heavens and the earth. He created day and night. God's power created vegetation. Then God, said, "Let the earth produce living creatures according to their kinds; livestock, creatures wildlife." Then God said, "Let us make man in our image, according to our likeness. They will rule the fish of the sea, the birds in the sky, livestock, the whole earth, and the creatures that crawl on the earth." So, God created man in his image; he created him in the image of God; he created them male and female.

This is the power and authority of God, Dr. Stanley explains. God is a sovereign God. He is above all other chiefs. God is supreme in power. He is our ruler and monarch. The following scriptures are proof of His character and His sovereignty. Another spiritual blessing of God's power and authority is that God knew us before we were born. God knows everything and is in control of everything.

Please read the following books of The Bible on the character of God:

Genesis
Daniels
Romans
Psalms
1 Chronicles
Ephesians
John

The main reason Jesus came to earth was to save you and me. Jesus Christ died on the cross paid the price for all our sins so that we may spend eternity with our Heavenly Father. Be thankful, be so very thankful today and every day for the person who knows everything and controls everything our Lord Jesus Christ. Who is God? He is our way maker, miracle worker, and our promise keeper.

God loves you, and this is His wish for you.

Dr. Charles Stanley – Sermon Notes – March 13, 2021 - THE FOREKNOWLEDGE OF GOD

Definition of Foreknowledge – knowing; to know of beforehand

Definition of Destination – the place toward which one is going or sent

Definition of Predestination – the doctrine that God foreordained everything that would happen; God predestines souls to salvation or damnation; one's destiny

Definition of Predestine – to destine beforehand

Definition of Destiny – one's fate

Definition of Damnation – a damning or being damned; hell

You may ask, "If God is our creator, is He also the cause of all things that happen?" The answer is yes. God reigns over all the universe, and there is no place in the universe where He is not present. God's attributes are He has no need and He goes to know one for counsel. God is our ruler and sustainer of the universe. God can not violate His self-imposed attributes. He cannot act unholy. God knows what's going to happen before it happens is it written in the Bible. Dr. Stanley says, Satan, fortunately, does not possess the attribute of foreknowledge.

God does not participate in any violation of the Bible, nor does He desire to make us violate the Bible. We cannot limit God's knowledge. He is wise or He is not God. Everything God does for us is through Jesus Christ. He is the Father for all of us if we are believers. Do you want to serve a God who is unaware of what is happening? God has a plan and relationship with the believers, not the non-believers.

> *For those He foreknew He also predestined to be conformed to the image of His Son, so that He would be the firstborn among many brothers.*
>
> — Romans 8:29

> *Blessed be the God and Father of our Lord Jesus Christ, who has blessed us with every spiritual blessing in the heavens, in Christ; for He chose us in Him, before the foundation of the world, to be holy and blameless in His sight. In love, He predestined us to be adopted through Jesus Christ for Himself, according to His favor and will, to the praise of His glorious grace that He favored us with in the Beloved.*
>
> — Ephesians 1:3-6

> *There is one body and one Spirit, just as you were called to one hope at your calling; one Lord, one faith, one baptism, one God and Father of all, who is above all and through all and in all. Now grace was given to each one of us according to the measure of the Messiah's gift.*
>
> — Ephesians 4:4-7

> *Therefore, be imitators of God, as dearly loved children. And walk in love, as the Messiah also loved us and gave Himself for us, a sacrificial and fragrant offering to God.*
>
> — Ephesians 5:1-2

God is self-existing, He is power, He is wise, and He is not dependent on anything. Dr. Stanley closed this sermon by saying, "We all get saved alike, by the grace of our loving God."

> *For everyone who calls on the name of the Lord will be saved.*
>
> — Romans 10:13

Today, you need to get on your knees in prayer and thanksgiving. Acknowledge that you believe in the foreknowledge of God and be grateful God is who He says He is — the one and only one ruler of the universe.

God loves you, and this is His wish for you.

**Dr. Charles Stanley – Sermon Notes – March 20, 2021
-THE FOREKNOWLEDGE OF GOD – Part 2**

Definition of Predestination – the doctrine that God foreordained everything that would happen; God predestines souls to salvation or damnation; one's destiny

Predestination, election, foreknowledge. These teachings have been the topics of seemingly endless debate and even disagreements among God's people. But what do these words mean? Do they matter outside a seminary classroom? The points and counterpoints about what God knows, who He chooses, and what man decides are all very complex. In this message, Dr. Stanley helps us examine some key truths from scripture, God's foreknowledge, and its relationship to predestination, election, and salvation.

> *For everyone who calls on the name of the Lord will be saved.*
>
> — Romans 10:13

We are all sinners, but we are saved by the grace of God, our Heavenly Father. He does not operate by drawing a line in the middle, cutting people out. We are all saved by the grace of God. He has the power and strength to open His arms to the whole world. God will put so much pressure on you that, eventually, you must obey. God is waiting for you to surrender to Him because that is how much He loves you and me.

For I am not ashamed of the gospel, because it is God's power for salvation to everyone who believes, first to the Jew, and also to the Greek. For in it God's righteousness is revealed from faith to faith, just as it is written: The righteous will live by faith.

— Romans 1:16-17

God will do the just thing. He makes no mistakes.

It is written in the Bible that God can not violate His self-imposed attributes and act unholy. God can not violate His character. God desires to have anyone and everyone's name written in the Book of Life.

For God loved the world in this way: He gave His One and Only Son, so that everyone who believes in Him will not perish but have eternal life.

— John 3:16

So, what is the plan and will of God? He does not exclude anyone. God is justice. His judgement is based on three criteria:

1.   The light and the truth that we possess.
2.   The opportunities we are given.
3.   The actions we take with the light and the opportunities provided.

God is the scorekeeper He knows everyone and everything. God does not cast out His people.

For the grace of God has appeared, with salvation for all people, instructing us to deny godlessness and worldly lusts and to live in a sensible, righteous, and godly way in the present age, while we wait for the blessed hope and the appearing of the glory of our great God and Savior, Jesus Christ. He gave Himself for us to redeem us from all lawlessness and to cleanse for Himself a special people, eager to do good works.

— Titus 2:11-14

We are saved by the pure grace of God. That is God's big plan for you and me. For everyone who calls on the name of the Lord shall be saved and have their name written in the Book of Life forever and ever. Please, do not miss out on this precious gift.

God loves you, and this is His wish for you.

104

Dr. Charles Stanley – Sermon Notes – March 27, 2021 – JESUS, THE SEEKING SAVIOR

When Jesus died on the cross, He wasn't just paying for the sins of the men who killed Him or those who stood and watched. He paid for the sins of all mankind. In this message, Dr. Stanley emphasizes how Jesus seeks out the heart of every lost man and woman.

God never turns away anyone. That is how much He loves and desires to have a relationship with us. He loves us so much that He died for us.

BEHOLD I STAND KNOCKING AT YOUR DOOR.

What do you do when God knocks on your door? Do you ignore his knocking and pretend you do not hear? Do you instantly say, "I'm saved so don't mess with me." Dr. Stanley warns us not to have a lukewarm relationship with God. If you hear God knocking, it's because He has something important to say. He knows what is coming for you, and this is His way of letting you know. God knocks until you let Him in. God wants your attention because it is for your own good. God will seek your attention through difficult times, pain, suffering, and hardship. It is His way of waking you up! God is a respectful deity. He respects your freedom to choose a relationship with Him or rejecting Him. Please, do not have a lukewarm relationship with God.

I know your works, that you are neither cold nor hot. I wish that you were cold or hot. So, because you are lukewarm, and neither hot nor cold, I am going to vomit you out of My mouth. Because you say, 'I'm rich; I have become wealthy, and need nothing,' and you don't know that you are wretched, pitiful, poor, blind, and naked, I advise you to buy from Me gold refined in the fire so that you may be rich, and white clothes so that you may be dressed and your shameful nakedness not be exposed, and ointment to spread on your eyes so that you may see. As many as I love, I rebuke and discipline. So be committed and repent. Listen! I stand at the door and knock. If anyone hears My voice and opens the door, I will come in to him and have dinner with him, and he with Me.

— Revelation 3:15-20

No one can come to Me unless the Father who sent Me draws him, and I will raise him up on the last day. It is written in the Prophets: And they will all be taught by God. Everyone who has listened to and learned from the Father comes to Me, not that anyone has seen the Father except the One who is from God. He has seen the Father.

— John 6:44-46

When God comes knocking at your heart, run to it as quickly as you can. God has something for you, and He is letting you in on the details of what to expect. It is a special assignment selected by God just for you. Do not turn a deaf ear to God when He says, "Behold, I stand knocking at your door." Jesus seeks out the heart of every lost man and woman, and He keeps knocking until you open the door.

God loves you, and this is His wish for you.

105

**Dr. Charles Stanley – Sermon Notes – April 1, 2021
– PREPARING FOR EASTER – JESUS SAYS**

Jesus demonstrated His strength on the road to Jerusalem. Jesus, the son of David, orchestrated His journey along with His disciples as they traveled there. He downplayed His actions to avoid drawing a crowd. Jesus was sick and weak as he rode a colt on this journey, but He showed love, mercy, kindness, and a tender heart.

> *There were two blind men sitting by the road. When they heard that Jesus was passing by, they cried out, "Lord, have mercy on us, Son of David!" The crowd told them to keep quiet, but they cried out all the more, "Lord, have mercy on us, Son of David!" Jesus stopped, called them, and said, "What do you want Me to do for you?" "Lord," they said to Him, "open our eyes!" Moved with compassion, Jesus touched their eyes. Immediately they could see, and they followed Him.*
>
> *– Matthew 20:30-34*

In this biblical story, one might think Jesus was riding a stallion. Jesus was in complete control, and even His disciples did not know upon their arrival if Jesus would be crowned or crucified.

> *A very large crowd spread their robes on the road; others were cutting branches from the trees and spreading them on the road. Then the crowds who went ahead of Him and those who followed kept shouting: Hosanna to the Son of David! Blessed is He who comes in the name*

*of the Lord! Hosanna in the highest heaven! When He
entered Jerusalem, the whole city was shaken, saying,
"Who is this?" And the crowds kept saying, "This is
the prophet Jesus from Nazareth in Galilee!"*

— Matthew 21:8-10

Once they arrived in Jerusalem, they immediately went to the
Temple — God's House — and Jesus instructed buyers, sellers, and
moneychangers to leave immediately! The crowd was mesmerized
by His appearance, power, and authority.

*Jesus went into the temple complex and drove out all
those buying and selling in the temple. He overturned
the money changers' tables and the chairs of those selling
doves. And He said to them, "It is written, My house
will be called a house of prayer. But you are making it
a den of thieves!"*

— Matthew 21:12-13

At Easter, we must honor and remember what Jesus did for us. He
paid the price for all our sins, so that we may have eternal life with
Him in heaven. Jesus did not even blame the men who crucified
Him, saying, "Father, forgive them, because they do not know
not what they are doing." That is how much He loves you and
me! Hosanna in the highest Heaven.

*"Peace, I leave with you. My peace I give to you. I do
not give to you as the world gives. Your heart must not
be troubled or fearful. You have heard Me tell you, 'I am
going away, and I am coming to you.' If you loved Me,
you would have rejoiced that I am going to the Father,
because the Father is greater than I. I have told you now
before it happens so that when it does happen you may
believe. I will not talk with you much longer, because the*

ruler of the world is coming. He has no power over Me. On the contrary, [I am going away] so that the world may know that I love the Father. Just as the Father commanded Me, so I do. "Get up; let's leave this place.
– John 14:27-31

God loves you, and this is His wish for you.

106

Dr. Charles Stanley – Sermon Notes – April 3, 2021 – THE CRUCIFIXION OF JESUS

If anyone asks you, 'Why are you untying it?' say this: 'The Lord needs it.' " So those who were sent left and found it just as He had told them. As they were untying the young donkey, its owners said to them, "Why are you untying the donkey?" "The Lord needs it," they said. Then they brought it to Jesus, and after throwing their robes on the donkey, they helped Jesus get on it. As He was going along, they were spreading their robes on the road. Now He came near the path down the Mount of Olives, and the whole crowd of the disciples began to praise God joyfully with a loud voice for all the miracles they had seen: Blessed is the King who comes in the name of the Lord. Peace in heaven and glory in the highest heaven!

– Luke 19:31-38

After two days it was the Passover and the Festival of Unleavened Bread. The chief priests and the scribes were looking for a treacherous way to arrest and kill Him. "Not during the festival," they said, "or there may be rioting among the people."

– Mark 14:1-2

Then Pilate took Jesus and had Him flogged. The soldiers also twisted together a crown of thorns, put it on His head, and threw a purple robe around Him. And they repeatedly came up to Him and said, "Hail, King of the Jews!" and were slapping His face. Pilate went outside again and said to them, "Look, I'm bringing Him outside to you to let you know I find no grounds for charging Him."

Then Jesus came out wearing the crown of thorns and the purple robe. Pilate said to them, "Here is the man!" When the chief priests and the temple police saw Him, they shouted, "Crucify! Crucify!" Pilate responded, "Take Him and crucify Him yourselves, for I find no grounds for charging Him."

"We have a law," the Jews replied to him, "and according to that law He must die, because He made Himself the Son of God." When Pilate heard this statement, he was more afraid than ever. He went back into the headquarters and asked Jesus, "Where are You from?" But Jesus did not give him an answer. So Pilate said to Him, "You're not talking to me? Don't You know that I have the authority to release You and the authority to crucify You?"

"You would have no authority over Me at all," Jesus answered him, "if it hadn't been given you from above. This is why the one who handed Me over to you has the greater sin." From that moment Pilate made every effort to release Him. But the Jews shouted, "If you release this man, you are not Caesar's friend. Anyone who makes himself a king opposes Caesar!" When Pilate heard these words, he brought Jesus outside. He sat down on the judge's bench in a place called the Stone Pavement.

– John 19:1-13

Who is the one who condemns? Christ Jesus is the One who died, but even more, has been raised; He also is at the right hand of God and intercedes for us. Who can separate us from the love of Christ? Can affliction or anguish or persecution or famine or nakedness or danger or sword?

— Romans 8:34-35

Therefore since we also have such a large cloud of witnesses surrounding us, let us lay aside every weight and the sin that so easily ensnares us, and run with endurance the race that lies before us, keeping our eyes on Jesus, the source and perfecter of our faith, who for the joy that lay before Him endured a cross and despised the shame, and has sat down at the right hand of God's throne.

— Hebrews 12:1-2

if you confess with your mouth, "Jesus is Lord," and believe in your heart that God raised Him from the dead, you will be saved.

— Romans 10:9

If we live, we live to the Lord; and if we die, we die to the Lord. Therefore, whether we live or die, we belong to the Lord. Christ died and came to life for this: that He might rule over both the dead and the living.

— Romans 14:8-9

And when you were dead in trespasses and in the uncircumcision of your flesh, He made you alive with Him and forgave us all our trespasses. He erased the certificate of debt, with its obligations, that was against

*us and opposed to us, and has taken it out of the way
by nailing it to the cross.*

— Colossians 2:13-14

*[My goal] is to know Him and the power of His
resurrection and the fellowship of His sufferings, being
conformed to His death, assuming that I will somehow
reach the resurrection from among the dead.*

— Philippians 3:10-11

*Now if we died with Christ, we believe that we will also
live with Him, because we know that Christ, having
been raised from the dead, no longer dies. Death no
longer rules over Him.*

— Romans 6:8-9

*When the Sabbath was over, Mary Magdalene, Mary
the mother of James, and Salome bought spices, so they
could go and anoint Him. Very early in the morning,
on the first day of the week, they went to the tomb at
sunrise. They were saying to one another, "Who will
roll away the stone from the entrance to the tomb for
us?" Looking up, they observed that the stone-which
was very large-had been rolled away. When they entered
the tomb, they saw a young man dressed in a long
white robe sitting on the right side; they were amazed
and alarmed. "Don't be alarmed," he told them. "You
are looking for Jesus the Nazarene, who was crucified.
He has been resurrected! He is not here! See the place
where they put Him. But go, tell His disciples and
Peter, 'He is going ahead of you to Galilee; you will see
Him there just as He told you.' So they went out and
started running from the tomb, because trembling and*

astonishment overwhelmed them. And they said nothing to anyone, since they were afraid.

Early on the first day of the week, after He had risen, He appeared first to Mary Magdalene, out of whom He had driven seven demons. She went and reported to those who had been with Him, as they were mourning and weeping. Yet, when they heard that He was alive and had been seen by her, they did not believe it. Then after this, He appeared in a different form to two of them walking on their way into the country. And they went and reported it to the rest, who did not believe them either.

Later, He appeared to the Eleven themselves as they were reclining at the table. He rebuked their unbelief and hardness of heart, because they did not believe those who saw Him after He had been resurrected. Then He said to them, "Go into all the world and preach the gospel to the whole creation. Whoever believes and is baptized will be saved, but whoever does not believe will be condemned. And these signs will accompany those who believe: In My name they will drive out demons; they will speak in new languages; they will pick up snakes; if they should drink anything deadly, it will never harm them; they will lay hands on the sick, and they will get well."

Then after speaking to them, the Lord Jesus was taken up into heaven and sat down at the right hand of God.
           — Mark 16:1-19

"Your heart must not be troubled. Believe in God; believe also in Me. In My Father's house are many dwelling places;, a traveler's resting place. The Gk word

is related to the verb meno, meaning remain or stay,
which occurs 40 times in John. if not, I would have told
you. I am going away to prepare a place for you. If I go
away and prepare a place for you, I will come back and
receive you to Myself, so that where I am you may be
also. You know the way where I am going."

"Lord," Thomas said, "we don't know where You're
going. How can we know the way?" Jesus told him, "I
am the way, the truth, and the life. No one comes to the
Father except through Me.

– John 14:1-6

Therefore, since we have been declared righteous by
faith, we have peace with God through our Lord Jesus
Christ. Also through Him, we have obtained access by
faith into this grace in which we stand, and we rejoice
in the hope of the glory of God. And not only that,
but we also rejoice in our afflictions, because we know
that affliction produces endurance, endurance produces
proven character, and proven character produces hope.
This hope does not disappoint, because God's love has
been poured out in our hearts through the Holy Spirit
who was given to us.

– Romans 5:1-5

After this I saw four angels standing at the four corners
of the earth, restraining the four winds of the earth so
that no wind could blow on the earth or on the sea or
on any tree. Then I saw another angel rise up from the
east, who had the seal of the living God. He cried out
in a loud voice to the four angels who were empowered
to harm the earth and the sea: "Don't harm the earth
or the sea or the trees until we seal the slaves of our God

on their foreheads." And I heard the number of those who were sealed:

144,000 sealed from every tribe of the sons of Israel: 12,000 sealed from the tribe of Judah, 12,000 from the tribe of Reuben, 12,000 from the tribe of Gad, 12,000 from the tribe of Asher, 12,000 from the tribe of Naphtali, 12,000 from the tribe of Manasseh, 12,000 from the tribe of Simeon, 12,000 from the tribe of Levi, 12,000 from the tribe of Issachar, 12,000 from the tribe of Zebulun, 12,000 from the tribe of Joseph, 12,000 sealed from the tribe of Benjamin.

— Revelation 7:1–8

Compiled by Linda Litchfield Strausheim

Printed in the United States
by Baker & Taylor Publisher Services